I Call You Friends

Timothy Radcliffe OP

continuum
LONDON • NEW YORK

Continuum
The Tower Building, 11 York Road, London SE1 7NX
370 Lexington Avenue, New York NY 10017-6503

First published 2001
Reprinted 2001 (twice)

Originally published in French under the title *Je Vous Appelle Amis*

ISBN: 0 8264 5188 8

Typeset by YHT, London
Printed and bound in Great Britain by TJ International Ltd,
Padstow, Cornwall

Contents

Introduction

This book centres around a question and a discovery. The question concerns the truth: Is the gospel true? Can I accept the teaching of the Church, and how does it relate to the truths of other faiths? This was the question that brought me to the Dominican Order, whose motto is 'Truth'. The discovery that I made in the Order was the centrality of friendship, the friendship that is the life of God and which we are called to share with each other.

These two themes are explored in the interviews conducted by Guillaume Goubert of *La Croix*, which form the first part of the book. It was a stimulating, though sometimes uncomfortable, experience to have my views on this and everything else probed by an intelligent French journalist!

The rest of the book consists of collected articles and lectures. Those in Part 2 focus on commitment. How can any of us make promises these days? What sense does it make to commit oneself to marriage or to be a member of a religious order? Part 3 looks at the meaning of mission in this multicultural world. What roles do men and women, Religious and lay people have in preaching the gospel today? The final part looks at a variety of issues such as: Is the teaching of the Church suffocating or liberating? How can we remember the horrors of the last world war, and especially the Holocaust, and still believe in God?, In what sense is the Bible true?, and What meaning have the sexual ethics of St Paul for today?

Timothy Radcliffe OP

About the Author

Timothy Radcliffe was born in 1945 and entered the Order of Preachers (the Dominicans) in 1965. He was educated at Oxford and Paris, and taught theology at Oxford. He was elected Master of the Dominicans in 1992 and since then has lived out of a suitcase, visiting the Order, which is present in 102 countries. He published *Sing a New Song* in 1999, and *Je vous appelle amis* in 2000, which won the French religious book prize for 2001.

Part One

Interviews

1

Childhood

Where were you born?

In London. It was the end of the Second World War, and my
mother was waiting for my father to leave the army.

Actually they were very sorry that I was born in London since it
meant that I wouldn't be able to play cricket for Yorkshire, which is
where my family came from.

What was your background?

My father's family returned to Catholicism about two hundred years
ago. Since then, most of my ancestors married into those old
Catholic families who had remained faithful to the Church
throughout the years of persecution. And I think that marked me:
I grew up with the memory of those martyrs for the Faith and a
sense that, however patriotic one might be, there is an allegiance
more fundamental than to the State; to one's faith. Later, when as a
young Dominican I was involved in the opposition to nuclear arms,
the question came up of breaking the law. Some members of my
family were rather shocked at the very thought, but it seemed to me
to be a family tradition. We had been breaking the law for centuries.

My father worked in the City. Actually, he was the first of my
forebears to have a job. They had land and devoted themselves to
the traditional English pursuits of cricket, hunting, shooting and
racing.

My mother's family were rather more exotic. They came to
England from Portugal at the beginning of the nineteenth century.
Her father was a General, and my imagination as a child was fed by
the diaries of his brother, also a General and an explorer, who

walked from Peking to Lhasa right in the middle of a Chinese civil war. Her family subscribed to *Country Life* for the Dalai Lama until he was exiled! Perhaps it was from my mother's family that I got a love for theology. My grandmother read people like Gilson and Maritain. When she was a child she bribed her elder brother with sweets to teach her Latin and Greek.

What atmosphere did you spend your childhood in?

It was the world of the English countryside. I grew up in a big house surrounded with gardens and woods. As children, we didn't feel wealthy: all our cousins seemed to be much better off than we were. But it was certainly a privileged childhood, and in some ways a very protected one.

We had no contact with industrial Britain. I had no idea what life was like in Liverpool, Manchester or Birmingham. I knew nothing about the world of unemployment, about the suffering of the poor. I remember my first Christmas after joining the Order, in 1965. I spent it with the working-class family of a Dominican in Liverpool. It was a real shock: an England of which I had known nothing.

What have you kept from your childhood?

First, the sense of belonging to a wide family. We were six children and there was an endless stream of cousins who came to stay. I sometimes thought my mother couldn't remember our names. But you knew you were loved without anyone having to tell you. You were a member of the tribe, and so I tell my African brethren that that is why I feel so much at home in that Continent! You knew who you were, who your cousins were, and their cousins too. That gave one a very solid sense of identity. This made things easier for me when I joined the large religious family of the Dominican Order. At the same time, it was a shock. It was a completely different world. People asked me, 'Who are you?' No one, till then, had asked me such a question! I had lived in the rather enclosed world of endless cousins who all knew each other.

Another important aspect of my childhood was growing up in the country. I learned to love the seasons of the year, the trees and animals. Much of my childhood was spent with my younger brothers in the woods, stalking animals, watching birds, trying to spot foxes, learning to be silent, to move without making the slightest noise. I think this love of nature has been important. In a way, it was the source of my earliest sense of God. For me, God was not associated primarily with churches, but much more with the contemplative silence of a walk in the woods.

Finally, I should say that our family life was a strange mixture of ritual and informality. We had to be formally dressed for meals. My grandfather wore a dinner-jacket for dinner every evening. It was a very formal way of life, with a great stress on the rituals of courtesy. But at the same time there was an informality, which came from my mother, who in her way is very egalitarian and unfussy. I think that in this way, too, it was a very good preparation for the religious life, which also combines ritual and informality.

What did you receive from your parents?

I realize today, rather late in life, how extraordinary my parents were: I never heard my parents argue. Never a word in anger, never. This must explain why I find violence and aggression so hard to cope with. My father was an utterly honest man. I simply cannot imagine him telling a lie, whereas I recognize that I sometimes find it hard to let tedious facts get in the way of a good story! Yet I aspire to become a man of truth, like him. In some ways that is what drew me to the Order, whose motto is *Veritas*, Truth.

He was a shy man. Like many Englishmen of his generation, he was not very good at expressing his feelings. That came as he grew older. When he retired from the City he went through a period of depression. He was lost, silent, and we did not know how to help him. What brought him out of it in the end was the Holy Week liturgy. I went to visit my parents on Easter Monday, and my father came to meet me at the bus stop. I watched him walking towards me and felt something had changed, there was a new spring in his step. 'What's happened?' I asked him, and he replied, 'I have lived Holy Week!'

As for my mother, what is remarkable is her absolute trust in God, the conviction that God will not abandon us: 'All manner of things shall be well.' Also there is her instinctive sense of the equal worth of everyone. In the village where she lives, everyone knows her because she talks to everyone. She is, as my father was too, totally incapable of snobbery.

You were born English. What did that mean for you?

I was born shortly before the independence of India (1 August 1947), at a moment that transformed an English or British sense of identity. In the past our identity has been given more by our relationship to other peoples, rather than by who we are in ourselves: the English being defined by our relationship to the Scots, Welsh and the Irish, and the British by the relationship to the Empire. That is the paradox of being an islander, that you do not have to define a discrete identity. It is not like being Flemish, for example. 'Why am I Flemish when just a few kilometres away they are French or Walloon? 'One is both cut off by the water, and so without the need to define oneself, and also joined to others by the sea, and so looking outwards. But now, after the loss of the Empire, and with more authority being devolved to Wales and Scotland, for the first time the English are asking themselves who they are.

Perhaps because of this English tendency to look outward, I've always enjoyed having foreign friends. The four grandparents of one of my best friends at school came from Hungary, Bolivia, Australia and India. I thought that was wonderful. In the same way, when I joined the Order, I loved the breadth of it: among my best friends in the early years were French, Mexican, German, American Dominicans, and so on.

Perhaps the English language is the most important thing about being English, for me. It's a wonderful, complex, subtle language. It's a melting-pot of languages with roots that are Latin, Celtic, Germanic, Nordic, French.

Today this language goes on being enriched from other sources: black Americans, Australians, Indians. The French often think of English as a language of technology and business, when more profoundly, it's a metaphorical language. In a discussion, the first thing Latins – especially Spaniards – look for is clarity. They want first to define the terms to be used. We English proceed more by metaphor, by allusion, by analogy. Clarity is not where we start from: it might perhaps be where we arrive at. So, what makes me English? A kind of attraction to those who are not English; an aversion to ideology; a love of language – I always travel with a book of poetry – the importance I give to friendship; love of the countryside and of animals. The English tend to find it easier to talk to animals than to people!

Did being a Catholic in England make you feel something of an outsider?

Yes and No. The English regard Catholicism with fascination and suspicion at the same time. Fascination because Catholicism is seen as mysterious and rather smart: there have always been conversions of rather grand people and of intellectuals. ... At the same time, there's a suspicion, because Catholicism is seen as foreign. Lots of English people cling to an idea of freedom at the heart of their identity. As they see it, Catholics give up this freedom to submit to a foreigner, the Pope. After the war, when a Catholic named Kirkpatrick was appointed a senior civil servant in the Foreign Office, the press immediately voiced the fear that he might receive instructions from the Pope in the confessional. This suspicion still lingers, although it's enormously diminished. I think Cardinal Hume had a lot to do with this.

One consequence of being in a minority has been to help Catholics to feel that they form 'one' community. It's a very mixed community: the old upper-class recusant families, middle-class converts, and a great many immigrant workers coming from Ireland. Poland, Italy ... All share a common identity that transcends class barriers. And that's unusual in England, where class allegiances are stronger than anywhere else in Europe.

What was your religious education like?

To tell you the truth, I have very little memory of a 'religious education'. I remember learning the Catechism by heart, but not much more. In fact my clearest early memories of religion are of Mass at home. Priests often stayed with us and celebrated the Eucharist just for the family. And then, every Sunday, we used to go to the nearby convent of nuns at Ascot for Benediction. The singing was magnificent. There were hundreds of candles. The great challenge for us as altar boys was to light them without knocking them over. The most important thing about the religion of my childhood was that we took it for granted. It was part of everyday life, the air we breathed. Going into a church was as ordinary as going into a shop. Praying to God was as ordinary an act as chatting with one's family.

Where did you go to school?

At Benedictine schools; first Worth, then Downside. The
Benedictines made a deep impression on me. They, too,
communicated a sense that one's religion was simply part of being
alive.

One of my great-uncles was a Benedictine – the one who was
bribed to teach my grandmother Latin and Greek – and he was so
evidently full of life and fun to be with: he loved laughter, food and
drink. The utter beauty of the Benedictine celebration of the liturgy
also touched me. I still have a very precise memory of the first time,
in the 1950s, when we celebrated Holy Week and Easter according
to the new rite – the darkness before we lit our candles, the drama of
the celebration of new life. The religion of my childhood was both
ordinary and magnificent at the same time.

Did you board at these schools?

Yes, from the age of eight to eighteen. For three-quarters of the
year, we were a long way from home. Looking back, this strikes me
as incredible, but it was what all our relatives did. We never guessed
at the time, but it was hard for my mother too. She drove us to the
door of the school, left us there as rapidly as possible, and, once she
was outside the gates, she wept. I was happy, but English boarding
schools were tough in those days and that was a shock for me. On
the second evening at school I was beaten for leaving my clothes on
the floor – not that I'm much better about that now! No-one had
ever hit me, no-one. I was utterly astonished that anyone might do
such a thing!

2

Vocation

How did you move from your childhood faith to an adult faith?

When I was at school, for all that I loved the beauty of the liturgy, I was in no way a pious boy. I wasn't at all a good example. I was the sort of boy who used climb over the wall to go to the pub to smoke and drink. I was nearly expelled after being caught reading *Lady Chatterley's Lover* during Benediction! I never stopped believing in God. That was part of the air I breathed, just as I never doubted the existence of trees or clouds. God's existence was obvious, but I didn't think about religion much.

I wanted to take a year off before going to university for some wider experience. I found a job in an office in London. There, for the first time, I made friends with non-Catholics, who posed hard questions about my faith, who asked why I believed in anything at all. This was a moment of real transition for me. I was faced for the first time with the question: Is my faith true? If it is true, then it's the most important thing in my life. If it's not true, then perhaps I ought to give it up. So it was emerging from a very protected Catholic environment and meeting non-Catholics that produced the shock that led me towards an adult faith.

Was it then that you realized you truly believed?

Not only did I believe, but that this faith must be central to my life. And it was at that time that I began to think about the Dominicans. In fact, all that I knew was that there was a religious Order whose motto was *Veritas*, Truth, but I did not remember which. I phoned a Benedictine friend who told me who they were and how to contact them. I made an appointment to see the Provincial. Within five minutes of meeting the first Dominican of my life, I told him that I wished to join the Order. That first meeting was a surprise, because the Provincial wanted to talk about football, whereas I had no interest in football at all, and was impatient to talk about theology. I went to visit the novitiate, at Woodchester, which deeply impressed me. I was struck by the simplicity of their life. The house was very dilapidated, with mushrooms growing on the ceiling of my guest-room. The second thing that struck me was their passion for discussion, about everything, from communism to the sacraments. For example, I remember a brother explaining how the sacramental life of the Church penetrates every aspect of our bodily life; it blesses our birth, death, eating and drinking, and our sexuality. No-one had ever talked to me in that way before about religion, and I was fascinated. When I left at the end of this visit, I asked to enter the Order. I asked the novice-master what I should read to prepare myself. I expected pious works of theology. He suggested Plato's *Dialogues*. In fact, they offer a wonderful preparation for the give and take of religious life! So for the next few weeks I read the New Testament on the train going in to work, and Plato on the way back.

Before these first meetings, had you really not had any contact with the Dominicans?

No. Though recently I discovered a deeper connection. One of my great-grandparents, George Lane-Fox, became a Catholic, and was immediately disinherited by his father. George came to Rome and entered the international novitiate in Santa Sabina,[1] where I now live. He appears to have been rather fond of escaping from the novitiate to go to restaurants with visiting relatives and it seems that the assistant novice-master suggested that he did not have a vocation, and so he left. That friar was Blessed Hyacinth Cormier, afterwards Master of the Order. So I may not have had much contact with the Order before I joined, but I appear to owe one eighth of my genetic make-up to an intervention of a Master of the Order!

Before you were nineteen, had you never thought of becoming a priest or religious?

No, never. Not that for me there was anything strange about priests or religious. I was close to many Benedictines. I didn't see them as creatures from another planet but as ordinary people who were my friends, and often my relations. But the idea of becoming a religious had never entered my mind.

Hadn't your Benedictine teachers, for example, ever suggested it?

No. Perhaps because I struck them as too unruly. . . .

What sort of job appealed to you when you were young?

Strangely enough I never thought much about how I might earn my living. However, I remember, when I must have been about ten, listening to a talk about planting trees to stop the advance of the Sahara. This struck me as wonderful, and for a while what I wished to do when I grew up was to be a forester. Later on I was attracted to publishing, and had lunch with the great Rupert Hart Davies to discuss it. So I was drawn both by the desire to plant trees to stop the desert and to cut them down to make books. I suppose that I have always wanted to have things both ways.

When you made this rather sudden decision to enter the religious life, had you felt a call from God?

I wouldn't put it like that. I believe deeply in the idea of vocation. I believe that all human beings are called by God. It is less a call to do something than a call to be. You can see in the Bible that the themes of creation and calling are very closely linked. Things exist because God has called them by their name. 'The Lord called me from the womb, from the body of my mother he named my name' (Isaiah 49.1). We are summoned to the fullness of life.

So I believe in the idea of a vocation. God calls. But it's not like hearing a telephone ring, picking it up and hearing God at the other end of the line saying, 'Come, Timothy.' It's infinitely more ontological; it's right in the depths of your being. So I didn't hear any voice, but neither did I just say to myself, 'Oh, that's a job I'd like to do.' I discovered how and who I was called to be.

How did those around you react?

My friends were really surprised, but my parents weren't. I have a very precise memory of the moment when I told my father. I was standing in the living-room, in front of the fireplace. My father was reading *The Financial Times*. He said, 'We'll support you whatever happens, whether you persevere or not. You must be free to try it and free to abandon it. We would not take that as a failure.' That was important: they gave me freedom. My father just suggested, to give me a good idea of the difficulties, that I talk to a friend of his, a well-known journalist who had tried the seminary but left.

I don't think my parents had any problem in me becoming a religious. Many of our friends and relatives were religious. My grandmother came from a family of nine or ten children, of whom seven were religious! On the other hand, they did find it a bit strange that I should become a Dominican.

Why?

In England, the Dominicans are regarded as 'left-wing'. They were very well known, for example, for their theological views, for the dialogue with Marxism. In the papers, on television, you saw Dominicans demonstrating against the Vietnam War, against apartheid in South Africa, against nuclear weapons. My parents were non-dogmatic Conservatives: they never liked Mrs Thatcher, but I think it was hard for them to see their son join an Order regarded as so far to the left.

Were you personally aware of this 'left-wing' reputation the Dominicans had?

It was not what drew me. I was attracted by the pursuit of truth, the poverty, the life of prayer and the brotherhood. But I had a shock when I joined the Order because I was the only novice from my background. I was endlessly teased. I was also given the impression that all of my family were exploiters of the working-class, immoral capitalists. That was very painful to me because I knew them to be good people, often holy people. So my first months were quite difficult.

Then the brethren began to refrain from these criticisms, and my own political views began to change, though not my opinion of my relatives' goodness! [*laughter*].

You went into religious life in the mid-1960s. So you took the vows of poverty, chastity and obedience totally against the current of that period, which proclaimed the consumer society, sexual liberation and radical challenge to authority. . . .

Yes, it is true that it was a very difficult time for the Order. Many left. Traditional religious life seemed to be crumbling away. We really had no idea of what the future would be; we even asked ourselves if there *was* a future. We were lucky to have excellent superiors. They couldn't see the future either, but they took the side of the young and gave us confidence. I remember a conversation with one old Dominican, Gervase Matthew, a famous scholar. I said to him, 'It must be very hard for you, Gervase, to see all this going on.' To which he replied, 'Oh, it was worse in the fourteenth century.' An historical perspective can relativize so many dramas. At the same time, that time of the disintegration of traditional religious life did force us to begin to reflect profoundly upon the essential nature of our vocation. We had to begin to rebuild our Dominican life, starting from the foundations, looking at how we conducted community meetings, how we prayed, what our vows meant, what it meant to study theology, how to preach. It was a time of great creativity. We made many mistakes, and often we ended up by discovering once again the wisdom of what we had previously rejected, the wisdom of the tradition. But those turbulent years were fruitful even if sometimes confusing and painful.

Let's take the poverty, chastity, obedience triptych in detail.

Poverty wasn't a problem. The Order was poor, and that generally struck us as very positive, though sometimes it was hard. I remember that when I arrived the Dominican students had thirty shillings [£1.50] pocket money a month, just enough for a few glasses of beer. We protested, saying, 'The priests get two pounds: it's not fair. Either we should have more or they should get less.' As you can imagine, we got more. But poverty gave us great freedom of heart and mind. When we travelled, some of us nearly always hitch-hiked. I hitched all over Europe, with an intense feeling of freedom. Personally, I took pleasure in the poverty, which was so different from my previous life. I remember once going to visit one of my uncles in Yorkshire. When it was time to leave, he asked me what time was my train. I explained that I was hitching back to Oxford. He wanted to pay for my ticket, but I refused. In the end, we reached a compromise: his chauffeur would drive me in the Rolls-Royce some distance away from the house and leave me to find a lift. When I spotted a good place to get a lift, I asked the chauffeur to stop. He handed me my bag, and a lorry picked me up. I found that mobility between two worlds – the Rolls and the lorry – liberating. It is the freedom of those who travel light.

Obedience?

I don't remember any difficulty in this area. In our tradition, obedience is closely linked to dialogue and fraternity. At Oxford I was blessed in having an extraordinary Prior for nine years: Fergus Kerr, who is a well-known theologian. He presided over the community meetings with immense wisdom. That was really a profound education in dialogue and responsibility for which I am grateful.

Finally, chastity?

That was the most difficult, it really was, because we received no formation in facing our sexuality. It was thought sufficient to tell us to have a cold shower and go for a run. It was even harder because we were not at all cut off from other young people. So we made mistakes. It took time, too, to rediscover together the value of chastity.

How would you define that value of chastity?

First of all, it gives us a wonderful freedom in the most literal sense of the word. These days, I spend a large part of the year travelling, visiting the Provinces of the Order. I couldn't do that if I had a family. I also think that chastity witnesses to the deep love that is friendship. 'There is no greater love than this: to lay down one's life for one's friends.' This is a friendship we live both inside and outside the Order. In the Gospels and in the Bible there are two models of love: passionate spousal love, in the Song of Songs and the Letter to the Ephesians, and then the love that is friendship, in John's Gospel. If we are to witness to the God who is love, then we need to find in the Church both ways of loving. We need married couples and religious, and, indeed, single people, who show differently the single mystery of love.

Don't you pay a high price for this freedom chastity brings?

I am convinced that what is the hardest aspect of chastity is not the lack of sexual activity but, much more, the lack of intimacy – knowing that you have a unique importance for one person who has that same importance for you. There was a time in my life, when I was about thirty, when I felt that very painfully. I can well remember dreaming of having a home, of having children, of hungering for that intimacy ... But in religious life I've also found joy, happiness, friendship, bursts of laughter, spontaneity and a way of loving that is extraordinary. I think this vocation calls one to the desert. The question is whether one dares to go into the desert, knowing that there, as the Bible says, God will speak to you tenderly. If it is really your vocation to go into the desert, you will find a real happiness there, a deep happiness.

You said that many left the Order. How do you explain the fact that you stayed in it?

I never doubted that it was my vocation to do so. What also helped me was that I fell in love with study, I discovered that I passionately loved studying the word of God. We have to be passionate: no-one can really live without passion. Combined with the discovery of the friendship among my brethren, I think that's what enabled me to survive, and more than merely survive. I knew that I couldn't be any happier doing anything else.

3

Further Education

How did your further education within the Order develop?

It began at Oxford, mainly at Blackfriars but also at the university, where I took a degree in theology. I had the good fortune to study with a Dominican called Cornelius Ernst. His father was Anglo-Dutch and Anglican. His mother was Sri-Lankan and a Buddhist. In his young days in Sri Lanka he was a communist until he was expelled from the party for his deviant views. He came to Cambridge to study and was a pupil of the philosopher Wittgenstein. He was one of the 'young Cambridge poets'. Eventually he had found that only Catholicism was big enough to combine his father's Anglicanism, his mother's Buddhism, the communism of his youth and the philosophy he had learned to love with Wittgenstein. He found his home in the Church. Cornelius played an extremely important part in my education. For almost six years we had a weekly tutorial – just the two of us. Once a month, I would buy a bottle of wine and we spent the evening together, talking about theology and listening to music. He was a man with an extraordinary breadth of vision and interest, symbolized by the opening words of one lecture, when he announced that he would consider the Prologue of St John's gospel in the light of later poetry of Rimbaud and recent mathematical theory! Not that I understood a word of it! He was not an easy man to understand; his writings are extremely dense. But he combined a deep sense of the Church and its tradition with a real sense of modernity and its questions. With him, I discovered that tradition and creativity need not be opposed. Two things were really formative for me at Oxford. First, the preaching of my brethren, especially Herbert McCabe. It is certainly from their sermons that I learned most of my theology. Their preaching demonstrated a great love for the detail of scripture; it taught one a concentrated attentiveness to the text. At the same time, in the English tradition, it was full of humour. That showed that seriousness and laughter are not incompatible. The second thing was the experience of having Cornelius and others as tutors. Each week you had to write an essay for your tutor and then defend your thesis. Studying did not consist in sitting down and listening to someone else talk; there was debate. At that time, at Oxford, this was my passion.

What memories do you have of the year you spent in Paris?

I had the privilege of living for a year with Yves Congar and Marie-Dominique Chenu, two of the fathers of the Vatican Council, at the Convent of Saint-Jacques. When I arrived, the first person I met was an old man who hugged me and pulled my hair. I thought it was some eccentric old friar. That evening, I discovered that it was the famous Marie-Dominique Chenu himself! His humanity touched me enormously, as did his sense of brotherhood and the absolute attention he paid to what others were thinking. He was a man possessed by joy, endlessly alert. He was always hungry to learn, to understand. Congar was certainly far more austere. But one could feel nothing but admiration for his passionate search for truth. One of the most extraordinary experiences of my life was going with him to Chartres. As I did a lot of translations for him, one day he said, 'To thank you, we are going to visit Chartres'. I pushed him around the Cathedral in his wheelchair, while he expounded the theology of the stained glass. In Paris, I became very interested in the works of Michel Foucault. I disagreed with him deeply, with his theory of the disintegration of the subject. I thought he was wrong, but in trying to discover why, I learned a lot.

You also spent some time in Jerusalem. . . .

Only six weeks, but I fell completely in love with Jerusalem. First of all, it is a meeting-place of people of different beliefs, the centre of the three great monotheistic religions. You can see this in the street, in how people are dressed, as Hassidic Jews, Muslims who have made the haj, Franciscans, Dominicans, Orthodox priests, Armenians etc. It is also the place where one is deeply struck by the reality of the Incarnation, which is not an abstract doctrine; it is the shocking belief that God became one of us, born in a particular place, at a particular time, in a particular culture. I was helped to see this by two different communities of the Order in Jerualem. Every day I went to the Ecole Biblique, where I got to know the great archaeologist Roland de Vaux, a wonderful scholar and a simple man. When he was invited to visit digs he took me with him and insisted that the archaeologists explain things in terms that I could understand. Here one saw the traces of salvation history being uncovered from the earth. And, secondly, I lived in Isaiah House, a community of the brethren engaged in dialogue with Judaism. Here I had my first encounter with our cousins in the faith, the Jewish community into which Jesus was born. It was a struggle reciting the psalms in Hebrew. I did learn to sing the Our Father in Hebrew, and can still just about manage it!

In 1971, after your solemn profession, you were ordained priest. Did you want to be?

I felt called to be a religious. I wanted to be a brother of my brethren. I was not very attracted to the priesthood, because I had – and still have – a sense of unease with any hint of clericalism. Some priests can give the impression of being superior to other people. I didn't feel superior to anyone, and I wasn't. The sort of distance that seemed to me then to go with priesthood made me uncomfortable. I accepted ordination because my brethren asked me to, because they thought it would be good for the mission. So I said yes: it was part of my obedience to the Order.

I gradually came to understand the joy of being a priest, first through the sacrament of reconciliation. One day, I asked Gervase Matthew, 'What's the most important thing you have ever done? Is it your book on Byzantine aesthetics, or your archaeological research in Ethiopia?' He replied, 'Hearing confessions.' I discovered that this was true. When you hear a confession, you come to realize that you are not a superior being handing out God's absolution to someone else. If you're really honest, you realize that other people's sins are sins you have committed yourself, or at least could easily have done so. The more other people open up their hearts and share their inner conflicts, the more you discover you are like them, a human being, weak and fragile, in need of healing and mercy. If the priest can offer words of encouragement, it's because those are the words he himself needs to hear. In confession, then, you can share God's mercy with other people, discover it with them, in the same pilgrimage of healing. As the years have gone by, I have also learned to love the celebration of the Eucharist. It's the moment – which has become central to my life and to my theology – when you enact the drama that is at the heart of God's relationship with humanity: God places himself in our hands as an absolute gift. The priest's role is not taking Jesus' place so as to become the focus of attention. In a way, the priest ought to disappear; in any case, he should not stand out and point to himself. He is there to help the re-enactment of the drama when Jesus surrenders himself entirely into our hands. It's a moment of generosity, of free gift, of pure vulnerability, and it never ceases to amaze me.

What did you do when you had finished your studies?

Cornelius Ernst wanted me to teach dogma. But I had studied without interruption since I was eight years old. I was sure that I couldn't be a good theologian without some pastoral experience. So I asked the Provincial to free me for a couple of years. I was invited to be a university chaplain in London, as assistant to a Benedictine in a team in which there was also a Jesuit and a Sister. But when I arrived, the Benedictine had been elected prior in Peru and the Jesuit had been summoned to another chaplaincy. So my first boss was a Sister. She taught me a lot through her humanity, her simplicity, her hospitality – in other words, all the things Dominicans are supposed to teach other people! As chaplain, I lived in a university hall of residence with 120 students. The only difference between us was that they had more money than I had. That experience was very formative. I arrived convinced that I knew how to preach, but I soon found out that my sermons did not connect with the students or they couldn't understand them. And it was through friendship with them that I began to learn how to preach. We used to have a drink after Mass, and they tore my sermons to shreds, explaining why I had got everything wrong ... They remained close friends. Two years ago, sixteen of them came to Santa Sabina.

Then the Regent of studies at Blackfriars, Simon Tugwell, asked me to return to Oxford to teach scripture. I protested. I was supposed to go and teach dogma and I had no special knowledge of scripture. He replied: 'You'll pick it up as you go along.' It's a very English approach: if you have a good intellectual formation, you can manage. So I had to plunge into teaching scripture, and did so for twelve years! I am profoundly grateful for all those years of living closely with the word of God. I studied it, meditated on it, wrestled with it, chewed it over every day. It was an unasked-for gift and blessing.

Did you write a thesis?

No, I went straight into teaching. There was no time to do a doctorate, and anyway doctorates were then not considered so indispensable as they are today.

What might you have liked to produce a thesis on?

There is one subject that fascinates me and on which I was planning to write a book when I was summoned here to Rome: the relationship between ways of doing theology and the historical and social context. Why is it that for Jesus, for example, the best way to do theology was to tell a parable, while for Paul it was to write a letter? Why is it that at a certain moment in the history of the Church, we had to find a new way of articulating our faith by writing Gospels? And why at another moment did we largely stop writing Gospels and begin to collect together the texts to make up the canon of New Testament? It's fascinating to examine how theology is always rooted in a particular cultural and social context.

4

Government

In 1988 you were elected English Provincial. How did you react to this responsibility?

Just before the election I had been feeling the need for a new challenge. I was coming to the end of two terms as Prior of Blackfriars, Oxford, and had been teaching for nearly thirteen years. I felt the need for something new, without quite knowing what. So I drafted a letter that I was going to send to the next Provincial asking him to find me a new mission. The only thing I hadn't imagined was that this new Provincial would be me. . . .

My first challenge was to get to know and love my own Province. I had always loved the universality of the Order. For me, being a Dominican was more linked with a sense of the whole Order rather than with my own small English Province. In fact, I did not know the Province well, and had had little contact with our communities in Manchester, Glasgow, Leicester . . . So the first challenge was to understand and come to love the work of the brethren of my own Province. I remember tramping around the parish in Newcastle with the parish priest and glimpsing for the first time the beauty of this ministry.

The hardest thing was giving up teaching. For twenty years, I had worked in libraries every day, wrestling with the word of God. I hadn't realized how far my studies had become part of my life and even of my prayer. I lost this regular immersion in silence, this meditative reflection. And then also the pleasure of teaching, the joy of opening the students' eyes to the Word of God. It was difficult to adapt to a life of travelling, answering letters, going to meetings. I was most nervous of having to assign the brethren to other communities, of asking a brother to leave one community, where perhaps he was happy and fulfilled, to go elsewhere, where he perhaps did not want to go. The brethren were very generous and affectionate, though. As they had elected me, they supported me. That's the advantage of a democratic system!

How do you govern a Province?

Government in the Dominican decision is highly democratic. I do not mean the party political democracy of Britain which is based upon the competition for power. Our democracy is based on the debate of the brethren in Chapter, in search of the common good. It is based on the search for consensus, even though one cannot always attain that!

And so the secret of good government is to create the conditions in which we really can talk to each other, and together arrive at a decision about the common good. This requires more than just voting on practical decisions. It implies a real understanding of each other, and of what matters most for each brother. Let me give just one example. When I was first elected Provincial, I had a feeling that the meetings of the Provincial Council were not running as smoothly as I hoped. Sometimes we could find it hard to reach agreement on quite minor practical matters, such as the renewal of a priory roof. I had the sense that our discussions were being muddied by deeper unresolved issues. So instead of just spending each meeting slogging through the agenda, we began meeting in the evening beforehand, for a much more informal discussion about what most concerned us, without taking any decisions at that point. Even if we did not always agree, at least we came to understand each other, and without that there can be no good government.

What initiatives do you particularly recall from those English years?

One example was the work we undertook with AIDS sufferers. That began in 1982, when I was Prior at Oxford. I had read in a newspaper that a young man had died in hospital of AIDS, absolutely alone. The staff were so afraid of contagion that his plate of food was left outside the door of his room. He had to get out of bed to go and fetch it himself. I was shocked to imagine someone facing death so alone. We decided that we must reflect upon how the Church could face this issue. It was a test for the Church: were we going to open our doors to those who were so rejected?

We organized a little conference to which we invited hospital chaplains, AIDS sufferers, doctors and nurses. We had expected about 40 people; 120 came. That was a good indication that there was a real need. I particularly remember the final Mass at the end of the conference. A young man with AIDS, named Benedict, came up to the altar to receive the kiss of peace from me. He then shared this kiss of peace with the rest of the congregation. At that time, people knew very little about the disease, and we wondered if we were all doomed! But we had broken the taboo.

Sometime later, someone with AIDS called to ask me if he could come and stay in the priory of Blackfriars to rest. I asked the Community and they gave me two answers: first, 'Yes'; secondly, 'You don't need to ask us again. Anyone who wants to come here is free to do. Whether they're suffering from AIDS or not is beside the point.' That made a deep impression on me; my brethren had opened their hearts to these most rejected people.

In 1992, when you were 46, the General Chapter held in Mexico chose you to be Master of the Order for nine years. How did that happen?

During the months preceding a General Chapter the delegates from the regions – Africa, Asia, North America etc – meet in order to consider possible candidates to be Master of the Order.

What does the term 'candidates' mean in this context?

They are those whom the electors decide ought to be considered for election. It would be completely contrary to our tradition for a brother to declare he wished to be considered as a candidate. I even think it's not a good thing to ask a brother beforehand if he would accept election. For us, accepting election is part of our obedience to our brethren. I knew that my name had come up in the course of these meetings, but I did not take it seriously. I thought I was too young, too disorganized, lacking in the necessary gravitas ... At the beginning of a General Chapter, the 'candidates' are interviewed by linguistic groups. I spoke a little French, a tiny bit of Spanish and no Italian, but I made them laugh.

The delegates identified three criteria: the future Master had to be in his second term as Provincial, have pastoral experience and know the Third World. Then the candidates were asked to make a speech putting forward their vision for the Order. When it came to my turn I refused. It seemed too much like a presidential campaign. I just said, 'I am in my first term. I have never worked in a parish. I have never lived in the Third World. I don't fulfil any of the three criteria.' And I stopped there. After his speech, each candidate had to leave the room so that the electors could discuss him. Almost immediately, someone came to tell me I could return, since no-one wished to say anything about me. I was a little disappointed. Even though I had no desire to be elected, I should have liked at least one person to speak up for me! But at the same time I was relieved.

The next day, we held the election. The role of electors is called in the order of the foundation of the Provinces – the Province of Spain, the Province of Toulouse etc. – until you get to the most recent foundations in eastern Europe and Asia – so one has a sense of the whole history of the Order. Very soon, it was clear that I might be elected. It was a strange moment; I felt an almost complete blank. My first words after being elected were to recall that, when a Dominican makes profession, he is asked, 'What do you seek?' And he responds, 'God's mercy and yours.' That's what I asked for then. It has always been granted me.

Nevertheless, when I arrived at Santa Sabina and walked past the portraits of the 83 previous successors of St Dominic, I suddenly felt overwhelmed, incapable, and that I ought not to have accepted. Finally I consoled myself with the thought that many of my predecessors had probably been mediocre and soon forgotten. I would do my best, and probably be forgotten too. My only prayer was that I would not be remembered for having been a spectacular failure!

How do you explain your election?

I have never asked that question. In a role like this one, if you become too self-conscious, wondering why one was elected and what people thought of one, then one would lose all spontaneity. It would be destructive. I think one has to cultivate a certain unself-consciousness, and just do what is to be done.

What does being Master of the Order entail?

There's no typical day. For two-thirds of the year I travel around the world visiting the provinces, meeting the brethren and members of the Dominican family, the friars, the contemplative nuns, the sisters and the Dominican laity. My role is to support them, particularly when they are living in difficult situations, confronted with violence, war, poverty and persecution. Our style of government tries to be as little interventionist as possible. When I visit a province, I meet each brother individually. I try to analyse what are the challenges the province faces; I don't set out to tell the brethren what to do, but to help them to assume full responsibility themselves.

When I'm in Rome I obviously spend a good deal of my time in meetings, and then I write letters; lots and lots of letters! Gradually, I'm finding out that letter writing is not primarily an administrative activity; it's always a pastoral and fraternal, and even theological, activity. Having taught St Paul for so long, I am finally beginning to understand letter writing as a way of doing theology!

When you visit the provinces, do you travel alone?

Never. I am usually accompanied by the assistant for the region concerned. The Order is divided into eight regions. For the large provinces, I would have two assistants. Of course, when I'm no longer Master of the Order, I'll have to learn again how to plan a journey, how to book plane tickets, get visas, change money. Nowadays, I can travel for weeks without a penny in my pockets, like a child or the Queen!

Which of your journeys has made the biggest impression on you?

First, Rwanda in 1993, at the beginning of the violence. Driving north, four or five times, we were stopped by road-blocks manned by armed and masked men. Every time, we were made to get out of the car, and I wondered whether this might be the end. I shall never forget one masked young man, holding my hand almost tenderly, swinging a machete, a haunting combination of tenderness and menace. What affected me most was visiting a clinic full of children who had lost their arms, their legs and their eyes from landmines. I remember one kid who took my hand and accompanied me around the wards, hopping on one leg. I went out into the bush and wept.

That evening we celebrated Mass with some sisters. I was conscious of having nothing to say in the face of such violence, but only something to do. When no words seem adequate, we can use ritual, gestures, words that have been given to us.

Another very important journey was to Iraq, in February 1998. That was a journey back towards our origins, to the land of Abraham. Just at the time of our visit there was the imminent threat of American and – I'm ashamed to say – British bombing.[2] I found that our Iraqi Dominican brothers and sisters were very little concerned with this threat of death; they were concerned with more basic questions: the truth of the gospel, God's final victory over evil. It seemed as though living with death for so long had confronted them with the most basic questions about the meaning of human existence. Despite the crisis, thousands came to listen to their teaching every week, driven by the same hunger for meaning. Never have I seen such a passion for God.

I also remember a Christmas in the Philippines, celebrated with lepers. There's a branch of the Dominican family, the Brothers of St Martin, who devote themselves to lepers and of whom many are themselves lepers. They celebrated Christmas by singing and dancing, with a deep joy.

I was particularly touched by meeting a woman who was a leper. She had lived all her life in a leper colony. For a long time, even after she was cured, she did not dare to go outside. She was afraid of what she might see in other people's eyes when they looked at her disfigured face. One day, she found the courage to begin to go and meet other lepers all over Asia to encourage them not to be afraid of going back into society. She is a true preacher!

Finally, I have a very moving memory of a big meeting, last year, with the Dominican family in Argentina: there were over a thousand people there. And it happened to be Malvinas Day! The streets were full of Argentine flags, with placards everywhere saying 'Down with the English!' Nevertheless, I was able to spend a very joyful day with my brothers and sisters. They gave me a most generous welcome, and had even put up a Union Jack for me! We celebrated Mass for all the dead, Argentinian and British.

What are the priorities for your term of office?

The priorities are set by the General Chapter. My priority is to implement what the brethren have decided. But I can tell you what my ongoing concerns are. First, to encourage the young, encourage their dreams. We should not use young people to plug holes, simply to keep going what is already in place . We need to give them space so that they can do new things and retain their enthusiasm and creativity. Then I must keep close to the Provincials; to share their difficulties and their concerns. I am there for them. We invite newly elected Provincials to each meeting of the General Council so that we can get to know them and let them know us. A third priority is study; seeking to strengthen our commitment to study. We need to allow young friars time to develop their intellectual gifts, and give themselves to theological research. Finally, to keep on stating that a simple and poor life is the only one that can bring us joy.

Have you ever felt that your brethren didn't understand you?

Never. First, because my prime obligation is to understand them. If there is a misunderstanding, I reckon that it is my responsibility to overcome it. I was nervous that my letter to the Order[3] – which touched on the subject of affectivity – in 1998, might have disconcerted some of my brethren. Talking about homosexuality, among other things, can be shocking in certain cultures. But I experienced no negative reactions. The brethren really tried to understand why we needed to talk more openly about such issues. I have never felt isolated.

5

History

Who are the figures in the history of the Order to whom you feel particularly attached?

The trouble is there are so many of them ... Dominic, of course, who was always one of the brethren. And then his immediate successor, Jordan of Saxony.[4] Elected very young, he didn't feel he was capable of governing: 'How can I govern the Order when I don't even know how to govern myself?' I often feel that. Jordan was a man filled with love. The letters he wrote to Blessed Diana d'Andalo[5] overflow with love, with a frankness and freshness I find wonderful. You find the similar relationship in the fourteenth century between Raymond of Capua, also a Master of the Order, and Catherine of Siena. We cannot think of them without the love they had for each other: Jordan and Diana; Raymond and Catherine.

I find Catherine of Siena immensely attractive: her courage; her amazing lack of fear, as in that famous letter written in 1375 to Pope Gregory IX, who was hesitating whether to leave Avignon and return Rome: 'Go on, do not be afraid. You have no right to be afraid.'

Albert the Great and Thomas Aquinas, because their holiness was closely linked to their intelligence. We tend to regard thinking as cold, abstract, cerebral. But for those thirteenth-century friars, loving God and one's neighbour were deeply linked: how do you love those whom you do not know and how do you know whom you do not love? Albert's boundless curiosity stands at the beginning of modern science, where wonder at the complexity of nature is linked with the praise of God. In our Church, which is so often split by ideology, Thomas is a wonderful example, always taking the position of his opponents seriously, setting out fairly the objections to his own position. He can teach us the meaning of dialogue. St Antoninus of Florence (1389–1459), who grappled with the moral issues raised by the post-medieval economic system. Bartolomé de Las Casas (1484–1566) who fought against the Spanish conquistadors for the rights and dignity of the Indians. Having begun by thinking that he was bringing Christ to them, he came to recognize in them the crucified and suffering Christ. And so many others: St Martin de Porres of Lima, with his closeness to the poor; Fra Angelico. The list goes on.

My final choice would be Marie-Joseph Lagrange, who founded the Ecole Biblique in Jerusalem, in 1890, and is one of the pioneers of all modern biblical study. He suffered a lot. He was attacked and condemned to silence, but he never felt any self-pity or bitterness. He kept his intellectual courage and his humility. He's a brother I should very much like to see beatified.

Has his cause been started?

It's even far advanced. It just needs the acceptance of a miracle.

In your opinion, which have been the brightest and the darkest periods in the history of the Order?

Certainly the thirteenth century was a wonderful time, with the enthusiasm of a young Order, that vitality of youth. Then the fifteenth century; the period of Fra Angelico, when the Order was caught up to an extraordinary extent in the ferment of the Renaissance. And then the period leading up to Vatican II, with so many theologians who contributed to that remarkable renewal – Yves-Marie Congar, Marie-Dominique Chenu, Edward Schillebeeckx, and so many others.[6] On the dark side, one cannot avoid mention of the Inquisition. The Order is often especially associated with the Inquisition. In fact, many other Orders were also involved. But no matter. I think the priority is to study what did happen. It is a highly complex matter. There were many different Inquisitions – the Roman Inquisition, the Spanish Inquisition etc. – which took very different forms. There were moments when the Inquisition was seen as benign and just, and others when it was clearly severe and cruel. That's why, at the General Chapter held in Bologna in

1998, we asked the historical Institute of the Order to investigate exactly what was the role of the Order in the Inquisition. That's where we have to begin. We accuse inquisitors of condemning people without a fair trial, and we often do the same thing with regard to the Inquisition, and so are guilty of exactly the same intolerance and prejudice with which we reproach them.

The actual birth of the Order, at the beginning of the thirteenth century, is associated with a frightening episode, the crusade against the Albigensians. Is that something difficult to live with?

Again, you would have to ask an historian. But in my view, the image of Dominic as a fanatical Inquisitor is a parody of the truth. Dominic never gave the slightest consent to the use of violence. He opposed the Catharist heresy with all his powers, because he believed that this heresy was poisoning the life of the people; not by violence but through preaching, through argument and through debate. Above all, he tried to be close to those he considered heretics. He shared their life, visited their communities, talked with them, listened to them and debated with them. The best-known story is that of an innkeeper who was converted after spending a whole night talking to Dominic. No, honestly; in my mind there is no deep link between the birth of the Order and the horrible destruction of the Albigensians.

Should the Church ask forgiveness for such acts of violence, even if they were committed in the name of the gospel?

Once the historical truth has been established, yes, I think so.

Many Catholics don't understand this notion of asking forgiveness. What does it mean?

We are asking God's forgiveness. Asking God's forgiveness means believing that God's grace can bring our lives, with all their failures, their sins, their sterility and negativity, to the Kingdom. Asking God's forgiveness for the Inquisition, for the Crusades, for anti-Semitism may seem strange, but it's bringing all that broken and sometimes sordid history to God, trusting that God will triumph over all evil. Asking forgiveness is not an attempt to forget what has happened; to wipe it out of our minds; it is daring to remember it, because we believe that God's grace is so creative that no act, however awful, can close the door to the future. It is an act of hope.

Asking forgiveness also means recognizing that I form one body with those who have gone before us. In the Eucharist, we celebrate that we are one community with the living and the dead, saints and sinners. If I want to be one with the saints, I have to accept that I am one with the sinners. I recognize that when I ask forgiveness for the past sins of the Church. Finally, asking forgiveness concerns not only the past but expresses hope for the future. Just as we ask forgiveness for what our ancestors in the Church have done, so we trust that those who come after us will ask forgiveness for what we do now. Are we really aware of what we, ourselves, are doing? I am sure that in centuries to come Christians will look back at us and see with astonishment our destruction of the environment and of each other. I trust they will ask forgiveness for our sins.

6

Identity

What is the Dominicans' special contribution to the life of the Church? What, ultimately, are they for?

What are the Dominicans for? That sounds a touch utilitarian to me. We are not for anything in precisely the sense in which a company might be for something; making lawn mowers or soft drinks. I mean to say, what are the French for? What we are for is clearly the preaching of the gospel but that is a purpose which is embedded in a way of life, a way of being. That way of life includes a number of ingredients, like a good stew: fraternity, common prayer, study, a form of government. All these elements produce a particular 'flavour', which I would sum up in the word 'friendship'. Other Dominicans would put it very differently, I am sure.

Central to the theology of St Thomas Aquinas was the friendship which is at the heart of God's life, a friendship which we are called to share. Personally, I believe that many of the distinctive elements of our way of life are marked by this idea of friendship. It is God's friendship and love that we preach; our life of fraternity is marked by it – and I do not mean just being pals! Our democratic form of government is not just a way of making decisions. It is an expression of friendship, our respect for the voice of each brother. Study for us is a way of growing in God's friendship, studying God's word.

Why do you say 'God's friendship', that friendship of Father, Son and Holy Spirit, when the word more often used is 'love'?

That's true: friendship may seem a strange word to use to speak about God's love. It can seem a bit cold compared to the usual vocabulary of passionate spousal love. But for the first Dominicans it revealed something crucial about love, perhaps under the influence of Aristotle, who had been rediscovered in the west around the time the Order was founded. St Thomas called friendship 'the most perfect form of love' because it is not possessive, because it values equality among persons, because one seeks only the good of the other. So it does illuminate some aspects of the divine love of the Trinity, the perfect equality of the Father, the Son and the Holy Spirit. This is an equality that we are called to practise as brethren in the Order.

How has your apostolate evolved over time?

All through the history of the Order, our study of the gospel and our preaching have had to face the challenge of new ways of seeing the world, new technologies, new intellectual tools. The invention of printing was a revolution for preaching. With books, the spread of knowledge was democratized: it changed the way in which we could share the gospel. We face a similar challenge with the Internet in this century. Or think of the impact of the new intellectual disciplines, such as psychology, sociology, anthropology, on our study of the Word of God and our understanding of the world. So these cultural transformations always face us with a double question: how to understand the word of God in the light of these new cultures, and how to understand these new cultures in the light of the word of God?

Also, for different generations the priorities will be different. At the time I joined the Order, great importance was attached to an invisible presence of preachers in the world. To carry the gospel to those who were far from the Church, and who often distrusted it, we had to be present in the world almost anonymously, sharing people's lives as silent witnesses to God. That was linked, in particular, with the attempt to bridge the gap between the working class and the Church, with the whole worker-priest movement. It was an extremely important phase in the evolution of our preaching. Nowadays, the young brethren aspire to a far more explicit preaching and identity. It is a new moment in the life of the Order which an older generation must understand and welcome.

This new generation one sees in the Church, which looks more clerical, more triumphalist – do you find it easy to accept?

I really have no difficulty in understanding a generation that attaches more importance to tradition. In England, we haven't the same polarization between traditionalism and creativity one often finds elsewhere in Europe. A French Dominican who, visiting Oxford at the end of the 1970s, said to me: 'I don't understand you English Dominicans; you go on street protests, you're politically committed, and at the same time you wear habits and sing the office, sometimes in Latin, and love the tradition. With us, it's one or the other.' Perhaps we do not attach so much importance to ideological coherence. I should even say that a bit of incoherence delights us!

Does that polarization you mention still affect the Order?

In the 1970s the cleavage between 'conservatives' and 'progressives' was very marked in many Provinces. It was very painful for us who give so much importance to unity. I think that split has been overcome more or less everywhere, or is in the course of being left behind. It needs to be, because opposition between right and left, between 'conservative' and 'progressive', is largely incompatible with the deepest institutions of Catholicism. The gospel and the tradition which we have received are always fresh and new. Where the question is still acute is in eastern Europe, where the debate couldn't take place earlier owing to oppression by the Communist régimes.

How do you move beyond such opposition?

It needs a lot of patience. First of all one needs a shared humility in the face of God's mystery. You have to listen to one another, see through each other's eyes, learn to value different opinions, fight against our tendency to label people.

Didn't one side or the other win?

The defeat of one side by the other would mean defeat of both. If you either destroy tradition or suppress creativity, it's destructive for everyone. One very important thing is to let the young be young, and not recruit them to fight the battles of a previous generation: if you give them the space, they will find a way beyond such polarizations.

The Dominican Order works on a democratic basis. Could that model of government be extended to the whole Church?

It's our form of government, and we don't seek to impose it on anyone else. However, this form of democracy expresses basic values that are important for the whole Church. In the first place, the value of listening to one another: our democracy is founded, above all, on attentiveness to one another in the search for the common good. This implies debate, of which, all too often, we in the Church are frightened. It implies taking serious account of my brother's objections, using our intelligence so that together we can find a unity beyond our disagreement, the larger truth where we can be one. Our democracy also expresses confidence. I have confidence in my brother. I may be in disagreement with him, but he has something to say. God, in a certain way, is speaking through his mouth. An extraordinary aspect of Dominic was that he trusted not only God but also his brethren. After the first General Chapter, he wished to resign because he had complete confidence in them. One of the roles of a superior is to keep nourishing that mutual trust.

Finally, our democracy means that we accept being vulnerable. When a Dominican makes his profession, he places himself in the hands of his brethren without knowing what they will do with him. This vulnerability, as I see it, is inherent in the life of the Church: it is Jesus' vulnerability in the hands of his disciples.

What relationships does the Order have with other religious Congregations?

For me it has a great pleasure to discover how diverse we all are, first in England, as President of the Conference of Major Religious Superiors, and then here in Rome, within the Union of General Superiors. In the past, often we did not resist the temptation of competition, but I think that time is past. I like to compare us to a tropical forest: there you find all sorts of animals – monkeys, parrots, tigers ... This diversity is necessary for the life of the jungle. In the Church, we need all the different forms of religious life: Franciscans, Carmelites, Jesuits, Augustinians, Dominicans ... It's an ecological balance and not like a competition between McDonald's and Burger King! I'm glad to see joint ventures developing, such as with the Franciscans in Geneva or with the Jesuits in Brussels. In Vietnam, we have a seminary where the rector is a Dominican while the two vice-rectors are a Franciscan and a Jesuit.

Do you find difficulties with the bishops in the dioceses in which the Order operates?

That's a big question! As we are present in over a hundred countries, we are in several hundred dioceses. I should say that, in the vast majority of cases, there are no difficulties. One of the keys to a good partnership is for us to be able to live a truly Dominican life, to offer our particular vocation for the local Church. Our vocation is not usually to run parishes. It may be so, especially when the local Church is being founded, and having some parishes can keep us in touch with the life of the local Church, but it should be the exception. It does happen that some bishops don't understand this, or want to avoid having any religious in their diocese at all, but that's rare.

And how are relations with the Vatican?

When I came to Rome, I did feel rather nervous at the thought of the relationships I should have with some Congregations of the Holy See. But it turned out to be easier than I expected. In the Vatican, as in any organization, including the Dominican Order, there are some individuals with whom it is easier to establish a relationship than with others. The important thing is to be straightforward, to say what one thinks, no more and no less. Some people are so intimidated by the Vatican that they say what they think the other person wishes to hear. Others are so suspicious that they arrive with all guns blazing. Neither of these is an adult reaction. The people we talk to are God's servants, like us. They deserve the respect and the openness we should hope to receive from them.

Do you see the Pope often?

I meet the Pope on various occasions: when he comes to Santa Sabina every year, on Ash Wednesday; on various occasions at the Angelicum[7]; when there are beatifications; sometimes in private. I am always astonished by how easy it is to speak freely to him. But I ask to see him only when absolutely necessary. I'm too conscious of the burden he must carry, of the incredible pressures on him. ...

Is the Pope the superior of the superior general of the Dominicans?

He is Bishop of Rome and the successor of Peter. I owe him loyalty and obedience, as does any member of the Church. From the start the Order has been closely associated with one fundamental element of the pontifical ministry: the universal mission of the Church. So we should be responsive to what the Pope asks of us. That is not a restriction of our liberty but our freedom for mission. For their part, the popes of recent centuries have always respected the autonomy of the Dominican Order. Well almost always: sometimes, especially in earlier centuries, popes sometimes tried to intervene, particularly to impose their candidates for the election of the Master. The brethren have always resisted fiercely!

It has also happened that some members of the Order have been affected by harsh decisions on the part of the Holy See. One only has to think of the worker-priests and of theologians such as Chenu, Congar and Schillebeeckx How did the Order cope with such actions?

They certainly produced deep sorrow and distress. For Congar, it was a time of terrible suffering. It is hard, when one has given one's life to the Church, to be treated with suspicion, as though one were an 'enemy'. But I think that men of such spiritual stature never doubted that the day would come when the Church would recognize what was true and valid in their teaching. Before his death, Congar was made a cardinal by John Paul II, and recognized as one of the fathers of the Second Vatican Council. Schillebeeckx enjoys a very high reputation in the Church, at least among those who have really read what he has written. ...

All we can do is search for and proclaim the truth to the best of our ability. We believe that the Holy Spirit was poured out on the Church at the time of Pentecost. If we cling to that conviction we needn't worry if our points of view are not accepted immediately. If they are true, they will be accepted in the end. If they are not, they will be forgotten. If I make a mistake, then the Church will not collapse. If you believe in this gift of the Holy Spirit, then one will not anxiously search through books of theology looking for heresy.

If the Holy Spirit has been given to us, the People of God will not easily be led into error. If God is with us, at the centre of our lives, we shall not betray what is at the heart of the gospel. We must not be afraid! The process of discernment, as to what is true to the gospel or not, is necessarily a slow one, and sometimes theologians will be condemned prematurely but rehabilitated later. It was quite some time before Thomas Aquinas was regarded as orthodox!

Are Dominicans, because of their boldness, still in trouble with the church authorities?

I am sometimes in touch with the Congregation for the Doctrine of the Faith about the theological views of some of our brethren. It has probably been like that ever since the Order was founded nearly 800 years ago. Sometimes we have been the Inquisitors, and sometimes those interrogated!

What does 'Rome' mean to you?

Many people tend to see Rome as the centre of a vast monolithic organization. That has not been my experience. Here one sees how truly multicultural is the Church, more pluriform than any other institution that I can imagine. At the Angelicum, for example, we have students of 98 nationalities. Here one meets every sort of theology, every variety of Catholicism.

I think that for some Dominicans Rome means, at least partly, Santa Sabina. Dominic lived here; Thomas Aquinas began writing his *Summa* here. Fra Angelico stayed here. Here we welcome members of the whole Dominican family. One day, in the refectory, an American Dominican asked, 'Do you drink wine every day?' A member of the community answered, 'Only when we have guests,' and added, 'I've lived here for six years and we never haven't had guests.'

Personally, I've come to be at home here. I hadn't expected to. When I left England I was afraid of losing my friends, of feeling rather isolated by my position. In fact, I've made the best friends of my life here. When I return from a journey, it's a joy to be home; I come back, above all, to my brothers and my own bed, my music, my books . . . and my computer.

7

Unity and Diversity

As the Order is present in over a hundred countries, and on all the continents, it is immersed in extremely diverse cultures. Is this diversity difficult to reconcile with the common Dominican identity?

It's not a difficulty, it's a challenge and a joy. The tension between unity and diversity has been part of the Order's life since the beginning. The first General Chapters dispatched the brethren to the ends of the then-known world. The first missionaries were sent to India in the thirteenth century. At the same time, the Order has always fought to remain united, unlike many other Orders which were split by disagreement. Hence the importance of the General Chapters, initially held every year to cement the unity of the Order and send us on mission.

An Order of preachers has to be united. If we are not, how can we be messengers of a Kingdom in which all human beings are reconciled? But we also preach a Word that becomes flesh in a variety of cultures. Jesus was a Jew, born in a particular time and culture. The Word must become flesh today, in Paris, in England, in Africa, in New York, in Calcutta. Preaching always implies inculturation. How do we cope with this tension between unity and diversity, remaining one and inculturation?

First of all, it takes time; time and patience to listen to one another. It also requires reflection, the effort to understand each other. I believe that inculturation need not fragment us. Diversity need not make us mutually incomprehensible. The more deeply a brother lets the Word penetrate him, to touch and transform all that he is, as African, Asian or English, then the more easily I will be able to recognize the working of God's grace in his life and feel close to him. In a truly African liturgy, for example, I can feel God's presence; God made flesh among us.

But we have to accept the fact that we live in a world characterized not only by diversity of cultures but also by inequality of power, a world in which the stamp of colonialism is still strong, culturally and economically. One cannot really tackle the question of unity without also facing that of power. The birth of a truly multicultural Order requires much more than simply being sympathetic towards another person's culture. We have to recognize that western countries intervene powerfully in the affairs of other nations, economically and culturally. I must be conscious of how that shades relationships within the Order. This implies a degree of self-criticism by us in the west.

There is a final challenge, which is that, for the first time in our history, we can no longer think of the Order as centred on Europe, but one which has many centres. In the globalized world the centre can be anywhere. We should, for example, develop south–south exchanges: What can Africa and Asia bring each other? We should, up to a point, evacuate the centre.

Up to what point?

For us, in a sense, Santa Sabina is, of course, the centre, but the members of the General Council are rarely here. I spend eight months of the year visiting the brethren. And this community is extremely multicultural: the fourteen members of the General Council are of fourteen different nationalities and from five continents. It's a good school for learning to live in unity and for discovering the fecundity of cultural diversity.

The question of diversity also affects all the forms preaching can take. How do Dominicans carry out their calling as preachers today?

For Dominic, preaching was proclamation of the gospel, however it was done. He preached in churches, in the streets; he debated with people in marketplace; he sent brethren to the universities to study and teach. So today, if we passionately wish to proclaim the gospel, we must use every possible means – teaching, writing, research, by our presence in university debates, and so on.

But preaching is not done just through words. There is a long line of Dominicans, starting with Fra Angelico, who have preached through art. This year we are organizing, here in Rome, an exhibition of painting and sculpture by contemporary Dominicans from all over the world. Another side of Dominic's preaching was expressed through his compassion. He was a man deeply touched by people's suffering. Being close to those who suffer is something deeply inscribed in our tradition. There are Dominicans who are prison chaplains, others who work in parishes, with prostitutes, with AIDS sufferers, with landless peasants in Brazil. In the last 30 years, the commitment to 'Justice and Peace' has become a major priority for the Order's preaching. I believe that our mission should always encompass these two elements: the word and compassion. When we speak, our message should always be compassionate. And our acts of compassion should always be a preaching, the proclamation of a word.

The Dominican Order also embraces another form of diversity. As general superior you are at the head of the 'Dominican family', which comprises besides 6500 friars and 4000 nuns, 35,000 Active Sisters and some 100,000 lay people linked to the Order. How does this family function?

The idea that the Order is a single family goes back to our origins. In the Basilica of Santa Sabina there are early inscriptions which refer to 'the Dominican family'. This sense of family is, I believe, intimately linked to our calling as preachers. Dominic preached the God who was made flesh, who became one of us, human. The preacher must be human to preach this human God. We learn to be human in our families. We are taught humanity by our parents, siblings, aunts and uncles. And so an Order devoted preaching a God who embraces our humanity needs to be a family that forms us as human preachers also; an Order which is exclusively male and celibate might not do that well.

We need to be a community that includes women, married people, lay men and women, with their wisdom and experience. From the start, Dominic saw this need. He founded women's monasteries as well as communities of friars. Today it's a major priority for the Order to reflect on our common mission with the contemplative nuns, the Sisters and the lay people: how can we together be preachers of the gospel?

The contemplative nuns are central to the life of the Order. They profess obedience to the Master. There is an international commission of nuns, which allows us to reflect with it on their vocation, and on their part in our mission. With the active 'apostolic' Sisters, we are at present going through a major evoluation. There are around 160 congregations affiliated to the Order, and new congregations frequently ask to be accepted. In the past, sometimes there was little reflection on the Dominican identity of congregations of sisters who wished to belong to our family. Today, our sisters are much keener to claim their full identity as Dominicans, sharing our charism as preachers. Three years ago, a loose federation, named Dominican Sisters International, was established, which re-groups most of the Dominican congregations of sisters. They elect a co-ordinating committee which regularly meets with the General Council of the friars. For the first time in the history of the Order, we can discuss and reflect together on our common mission. It's a very important breakthrough.

The Dominican laity are also living through a moment of transition. The lay fraternities, who used to be called 'tertiaries', have always been, and will be, an important part of the life of the Order. This is in no way threatened by the emergence of other ways in which lay people can belong to the family. A movement of Dominican Youth has recently been created and spread throughout the world, and we have just launched an organization of volunteers, young people who will commit themselves full-time to the Order's mission outside their native country for a limited period.

How can our men and women religious and lay people all 'be one'? We're in a period of transition. Until now our focus of unity within the Dominican family has been the Master of the Order and of the friars. Will this be the best model in the future, now that we are beginning to appreciate more the dignity of women and lay people in the life of the Church? We don't know yet.

Can you envisage Sisters and lay people as part of the General Council of the Order one day?

The General Council is part of the government of the friars. It would be strange for Sisters and lay people to be members of it.

One can't help being struck by the invisibility of women religious in the life of the Church. Leaving the question of priesthood aside, how do you explain so little responsibility being given to them, either in the Holy See or in Bishops' Conferences?

It really is a priority to see to it that women have a voice at all levels of responsibility within the Church. We are just at the beginning of exploring how this may happen.

The question I am most concerned with, talking about our Dominican Sisters, is how to respond to the desire of many sisters to be fully our partners in preaching. By preaching, I don't mean only communicating information about God. It is sharing a word of life. It is hard to offer a word of life if we exclude women, who play such an important role in the transmission of life. Our theology will be ill-adapted for the third millennium if it is not enriched with the wisdom of women. The purpose of preaching is also to break down barriers, the barriers that keep us apart from one another. In a way, this includes the barriers that separate men from women.

Canon law does not allow women to preach during the celebration of the Eucharist. But I don't see that as a major problem. As I said just now, Dominic preached in the streets, during meals, during Vespers, through teaching and debate, and in many other ways.

8

The Future

Is the Order going through a vocations crisis?

I would not say so. At the moment, more than one friar in six is in formation. I would prefer this to be one in four, but it is not bad. We have a good number of vocations, even in the western world. For example, there are many young men joining the Order in the United States, in France, Germany, England and Poland. Other Provinces – Italy, French-speaking Belgium, Canada – are beginning to show signs of recovery. The situation is more worrying in Ireland, Holland, Flemish-speaking Belgium and Spain. The encounter with the culture, if one can call it that, of consumerism tends to produce a crisis for the Church and for vocations to religious life, especially if the country has suffered from real poverty. Then, wealth can be highly seductive, but not for long. I do not believe that any society can stifle the thirst for God for long. So in France, England and Germany we lived through the lean years for vocations in the seventies, but now there are again young men who come to the Order. I would not be surprised if the same thing happens in countries which now have a vocations crisis.

Of course, everywhere the thirst for God and the interest in spirituality remains. The young often do not look to Christianity to satisfy this longing, but to the East, New Age and other more exotic doctrines. The longing is real, though sometimes it is marked by a sort of religious consumerism, cooking up a religion that suits me, that satisfies my needs. A little Zen today and some aromatherapy tomorrow. Ultimately, satisfying that thirst for God, which we all have, calls us beyond a religion that satisfies our needs, learning to hear the voice which calls me beyond myself to find my centre in God. It's like falling in love: if I love a girl because she satisfies my needs, that's not, at the end of the day, a mature love. That person is just a function of my little self-centred world. I discover what love is when I let her be the centre of the world and not myself.

How can you encourage vocations?

The first thing is to believe in religious life, especially when it goes against the grain of the values of our age. It *is* a wonderful life! We must be bold enough to say to a young man, 'Why don't you become a Dominican?' We dare to make that invitation because we believe in our vocation. The gospel must be preached. But two words of caution: we must not seek vocations just to ensure the survival of our own institutions. That is not a good reason for a young man to join us. Secondly, more important than gaining recruits for the Order is helping the young to discover what is their vocation. What is God calling them to do and to be? If that happens to be to be a Dominican, then that is wonderful.

What will the Order look like by the mid-twenty-first century?

It will be younger and less white. In Africa, one friar in two is in initial formation; in Asia and Latin America, it is one in four. Until quite recently, two-thirds of friars came from the western world. At the present time, almost two-thirds of vocations come from outside the western world.

It will also be a more mobile Order. The young who join us today often have a global sense of mission. They are much less tempted by provincialism. More and more, there will be friars who will, for example, be teaching for one half of the year in Latin America and the other half in Africa or Asia. The Internet will create other forms of community besides the priory, in which we can build community with people who are on the other side of the globe. But we must be careful not to identify ourselves with, in the words of a French Dominican, Gabriel Nissim, *le lointain semblable* (the far away person who is like me) and neglect the *prochain différent* (the neighbour who is different).

What developments do you regard as priorities for the Order over the next decades?

The word of God is central to our lives as Christians, as religious, and as preachers. So I should hope that a good number of young friars will devote themselves to the study and the teaching of scripture, constantly renewing their love for it, and helping us to hear what it is saying to us today. Every Dominican community ought to have a Bible scholar at its heart. That's essential for the whole of our mission.

We should also develop our presence in universities – whether as lecturers or as chaplains it is of little matter. That's where many young people are looking for meaning for their lives. We should be there to listen to them, to discuss with them, to be at their side.

Then we should take a greater part in the debates of our society. There are so many new ethical problems emerging, particularly with the development of biotechnology. I am delighted to see many young Dominicans undertaking studies in those fields. But that's not enough: we need to roll up our sleeves and throw ourselves into public debate. The Church, from time to time, intervenes by publishing a declaration on these issues. We need to go further than that, to take a real part in the debate. Finally, we need to find new ways of getting in touch with people who never come near a church. This is done, no doubt, by what is called, a bit pompously, 'the evangelization of culture'. In this western society, which is nervous of people who explicitly talk about God, then maybe beauty can touch them and help them to have a glimpse of the mystery of God. We need, more than ever, friars who preach through art. I recently met a Spanish friar who was learning mime. He told me he wanted to preach with his whole body, with his every movement.

Does a presence on the Internet strike you as a priority?

The last General Chapter, in Bologna, asked me to appoint a friar for the promotion of preaching through the Internet. Dominic sent his friars out to preach where people were; where they meet to relax, discuss, form community. Now, for many young people, the meeting place is the World Wide Web, so we must be there. The Internet is also a place for education, particularly for those who cannot go to university due to lack of time, money or qualifications. The Internet can give them access to knowledge. We have to be present on it as teachers. So the province of Toulouse has set up

Domuni, a sort of university on the Internet, with several hundred students. Three other provinces are now associated with it, teaching in French, English and Spanish. But you have to recognize the limitations of the Internet. First, because a very large portion of humanity does not have a computer or a telephone line. But also because preaching and education imply communication between people. The Internet is interactive in a limited way. When one teaches, it is good to see one's students, see what makes them smile or look puzzled, when they wake up and when they sleep. That's hardly possible through a computer screen, at least not yet. . . .

You use the word 'mission' often. What do you think it means in today's world?

A lovely name for Jesus is 'Emmanuel', which means 'God with us'. Our mission is to heal our split and fractured world, so that it is a place in which God can live and share our lives: 'God with us'. Ultimately, this is the Kingdom of God and the Kingdom comes as a gift, but our mission is a preparation for its coming, welcoming the gift. The word 'ecumenism', which we use for the quest for unity with other Christian confessions, comes from the Greek *oikos*, or house. Dialogue with other Christians is the building of this common home, God's home.

A missionary is not someone who goes to those who live in outer darkness and ignorance. God is already there before us. We seek partners in building God's home with us. This can happen in wonderful and unexpected ways. Our Japanese brother Oshida founded a Christian community in the hill near Mt Fuji. In the garden he set up a statue of the Buddha, with the child Jesus on his lap. The villagers began to come discreetly during the night to leave offerings. A place was coming to be where people of different faiths could gather and prepare for the Kingdom.

What are the main 'mission territories' today?

Another vast question! First, Asia, the continent in which more than half of humanity lives, has the lowest percentage of Christians. We go there to preach Christ but also to learn about God, here in the birthplace of most of the world's religions. The meeting of east and west is an enormous challenge for the Church's mission, but will be profoundly fruitful. The second priority is Europe, because it is the continent most crucified by the loss of meaning. If you will forgive such a broad generalization, in Europe one sees an enormous crisis of wisdom, of any sense of the ultimate purpose of human life. We have information but not wisdom. In eastern Europe, the crisis of meaning is particularly evident in the desert of post-communism. Freedom has at last come, but for what purpose? The priority is to go out to those who are suffering most from this loss of meaning: the long-term unemployed, the underclass in the big cities, those suffering from AIDS, and so on. Perhaps this crisis of meaning most deeply affects many young people, whose future is before them, but for what purpose, what end? Another challenge for the Church is to engage in dialogue those who are committed to the search for meaning but find it elsewhere: whether intellectuals, philosophers, artists, politicians. The preaching of the gospel is rarely just a proclamation of a word, from above or outside. We have to discover what is to be said in dialogue with those who are also searching.

Who is called to mission? Is it something just for priests, or for religious and lay people also?

To be a missionary is, in the literal sense of the word, 'to be sent'. We are all sent by God. We may be sent to some remote country to preach the gospel. We may be sent to those who are close – our spouse, our children, the people we work with. We all are called to bear a word of hope, to overcome the boundaries that divide us and to build communion. I remember an old Dominican sister called Sister Dominic. At the age of 80 she discovered a new mission, to be with those dying of AIDS. She was sent to people who wanted nothing to do with the Church, made new friendships, shared their lives. She told me, 'I've learned to dance at the age of 85!' She was a missionary with her whole being, out of compassion and love.

For an Order like the Dominicans, does tackling new mission territories mean leaving apostolates inherited from the past? Should you leave magnificent convents such as Santa Maria Novella in Florence in order to devote greater efforts to Asia or to street children?

You ask what we should close. I think the first question we need to ask is what we should open. Let's first do something new and then see what, as a consequence, we must give up. You mention the example of Santa Maria Novella, that wonderful priory in Florence, filled with Renaissance frescoes. It is true that we cannot let ourselves become museum keepers for tourists. But surely we can find ways of preaching the gospel through the beauty of such places. Beauty too can be a revelation of God. So I do not believe that we should give up all the monuments of the past. To take a modern example, I love the convent of L'Arbresle, near Lyons, designed in the 1950s by Le Corbusier. Every year thousands of architects come to visit it. It's a place that preaches.

In April 1994, in a letter to the Dominican Order, you wrote: 'All over the world, we are summoned to dialogue with Islam. Are we ready to give our lives for it?' Two years later, a Dominican, Mgr Pierre Claverie, Bishop of Oran, was murdered in Algeria. Does the mission need martyrs?

I do not wish for anyone's death. When I think of those of our brothers and sisters who live in situations of danger, such as in Brazil, where they defend human rights, I pray that they will be safe. But if it happens that they are killed, I give thanks to God, not that they died, but that they gave their lives. Martyrdom is the ultimate generosity. May we all be generous enough to give all that is asked of us, even our lives. Martyrdom shows that survival is not the ultimate value. We live in a society obsessed with survival. We take pills to make it to tomorrow, we're afraid of illness, of death. But is surviving such a deeply important matter? The gospel says, 'Unless a grain of wheat falls into the earth and dies, it remains just a single grain; but if it dies, it bears much fruit' (John 12:24).

9

Truth

'Veritas': What does the motto that drew you to the Dominican Order mean? What is this truth?

I think, first of all, we have to try to understand why the idea of truth is so suspect for many people. It can appear cold, cerebral and even arrogant: 'We have the truth.' Humanity, in the century which has just finished, was crucified by ideologies which claimed to possess the truth: Communism, Nazism, scientism and, today, consumerism. So we shouldn't be surprised if people suspect anyone who claims to own the truth. In this context, it's even more important for us to have the right sort of confidence in the proclamation of the truth.

But what does this mean? At the time of the 1995 General Chapter in Caleruega, we spent three weeks in Dominic's birthplace, in the dusty plains of northern Castile. I really had wondered how we would survive for so long in the middle of nowhere. But I fell in love with the place. More precisely, I fell in love with the light that pervades everything, its clarity, its luminosity. I believe that this light is typical of Dominic, his ability to see clearly, to recognize people's humanity, their goodness, their suffering. Truth is perhaps, in the first place, a light that reveals the beauty and goodness of God's world, and also its suffering and pain.

For this reason there is a close link between truth and love. This may seem strange, since we usually think of love as a nice warm feeling and nothing to do with the mind. But loving another person includes trying to understand who he or she really is. Growing in love implies coming to understand them, see through their eyes, penetrate their humanity; and growth in understanding overflows in love. Our contemporaries tend to think of knowledge as cold, an impersonal detachment, observing a distance. The Bible suggests otherwise: the word 'know' means a most intimate, indeed a sexual, relationship. Knowledge implies intimacy. Love helps me to know the truth, and the truth helps me to love.

Truth also opens up communion between people who are divided. When I disagree with someone, we can overcome our differences by looking for the larger truth that embraces my little truth and that of the other. The search for the truth means that we need not be stuck forever in our failure to agree, our mutual miscomprehension. Belief that it is possible to arrive at the truth, the objective truth, implies the promise of reconciliation, arriving at a clarity of perception in which we recognize and understand what is true for the other. There is no reconciliation without truth, as they discovered in South Africa. Take the example of the Balkans, those centuries of conflict between Serbs and Croats. What peace can there ever be, if they do not attain some common truth, some shared perception of their history, in which the sufferings of all the people find some objective recognition.

Affirming the possibility of attaining the truth is also an assertion of human dignity. We are made for truth, we look for it instinctively, even when we deny it can be attained. Fish have need of water, plants have need of earth, we have need of truth. I believe that we preachers have a tendency to underestimate this universal aspiration to truth, to underestimate the perceptiveness of those who listen to our sermons. Instinctively, they know perfectly well whether we are speaking truthfully or just spouting words.

But what is this truth? How can you define it, at least approximately?

When all is said and done truth for which we hunger is God, who has made everything and to whom everything returns. As Augustine said, our hearts are restless until they rest in God. God reveals himself to us in the person of Christ. Having made that bald statement, we must also acquire a certain humility in the face of this truth, which remains beyond our grasp. This truth is both revealed and yet beyond us. We cannot master it, or simply take possession of it. Thomas Aquinas stated – and this is at the very heart of his theology – 'What God is, we cannot say.' Words cannot enclose God; they can only let us approach the edge of the mystery. We can say true things about God. For example, I can say that God is good, that God is one, that Christ is risen from the dead . . . but we cannot know fully what that means. I cannot know what it means for God to be God. There is a paradox in our Dominican spirituality, a tension I find very inspiring: we claim friendship with God, but this friend is the One who is beyond words.

And yet, is it not the purpose of the magisterium, the teaching arm of the Church, that is, to state what the truth is, to define who is a heretic and who isn't?

I repeat: to say that God is beyond our understanding does not mean that no statement of the truth is possible. If someone says that Jesus did not exist, that he did not rise from the dead, I believe that he is wrong: I can make statements that are true, but I cannot wrap it all up. Heresy begins precisely when someone claims to know the whole of the truth. Heresy consists in trying to shut God up in a box, to reduce him to my little grasp of the truth. Dogma, conversely, seeks to loosen our possessive little grip, so that truth may disclose itself as ever more: as Augustine said, 'God is always more.' Dogma propels me on a journey towards the truth. I am well aware that in contemporary usage 'dogmatic' means just the opposite of this. But that's a misunderstanding.

Can you put two statements such as 'Jesus existed' and 'Jesus rose from the dead' on the same level? In our human understanding, the degree of certainty, surely, is not the same. . . .

That Jesus existed is an historical fact, in the same sense as the existence of Julius Caesar. We know what might count as evidence for it. When I claim that Jesus rose from the dead, it's not so simple. The resurrection is a mystery whose significance I don't fully understand. I can claim that there are historical traces of this mystery: the tomb was empty. If Jesus' body had been found in the tomb, the statement would not be true. So the resurrection implies historical facts, even if it cannot be reduced to one. We might be tempted to think of the resurrection as just another historical fact of the same sort as Jesus' birth, because we have a narrow view of what it means to be bodily. Many of the most fundamental Catholic doctrines are linked to our bodiliness: the body of a newborn child in the manger; the Eucharist as the gift of a body; the resurrection of

Christ's body, our own resurrection. I believe much confusion about Catholic teaching comes from our tendency to regard the human body as just a bag of flesh and bone. But the body is much more than that. It is my presence to other people: being bodily is how I am in communion with others. At the same time, it imposes all sorts of limitations: if I am in the next-door room, I cannot be in here with you; if someone is dead, I can't talk to him. The resurrection of the body is therefore much more than a corpse coming back to life. It is the transfiguration of Christ's presence to us, breaking through all the barriers that our experience of corporeality imposes. Perhaps one way of thinking of the resurrection would be to see it as the transformation of Christ into pure communion. So the truth of the resurrection is, in a sense, an historical truth, but it is more than that.

Are Christians the only ones who hold the truth about God and humanity?

In the letter to the Ephesians, one of Paul's favourite words is *pleroma*. That's a lovely Greek word meaning 'fullness'. Paul declares that the fullness of God has been revealed in Christ. I believe that. But we are only at the beginning of understanding that fullness of truth. It is manifested in Christ, yes, but that does not mean that we have managed to grasp it. We are and will always be on the way towards doing so. We do so only as we are ourselves transformed, and become more Christ-like. Knowing implies being.

For example, our Church is largely western. We are the product of a particular history. To a large extent, our faith has been defined in response to particular heresies. We need to engage in dialogue with other cultures and other religions in order to move beyond the limits of our European identity and become more fully Catholic. Catholic means universal. We shall never be Catholic enough!

We are Roman Catholics, and I love the tension between those two words. We are Roman because we are a particular community with its place in history: we are this people with this history. And that's fine: Jesus himself was born in a particular place, at a particular moment, in a particular culture. But at the same time we are Catholic, and this is why we always pushed beyond the limits of our present identity. This is the beauty of the history of the Church; when it left Jerusalem and moved into the Roman world, that was a transformation we can barely imagine, just as when it moved beyond the boundaries of the Roman Empire to embrace the barbarians. Each stage was a step towards the fullness of Catholicism. Each stage was a little death to an old and more limited identity, and a rebirth. We have to carry on this pilgrimage towards a truth we do not fully grasp. That's why we are attentive to other religions; not just out of good manners or a spirit of dialogue, but because they may be able to help us on our journey towards the truth of Christ. A Buddhist will have something to teach me about transcending the demands of my ego. A Muslim will have something to show me about the absoluteness of God.

Let's go back to the question of the magisterium for a moment. The organs of the Holy See nowadays have a growing tendency to use the expression 'definitive truth' to designate points of doctrine that do not always seem to be of prime importance. Is this notion of 'definitive truth' compatible with your description of a truth that is always still to be found?

Certain truths are clearly 'definitive'. Theology's unceasing work of exploration does not mean that nothing is sure. The Church has, for example, defined Jesus as truly God and truly human. It cannot go back on this and say, 'We're sorry, but after all Jesus is not God!' But theology has to go on exploring these 'definitive truths'. They remain provocative, literally, in that they summon us deeper into the mystery. We have to go on seeking what it means to say Jesus is truly God and truly human. That will go on until we find ourselves face to face with God – and perhaps even after! A theologian once said that all the Church's teachings are good news, but we have to find out why. The preacher's task is to make the liberating dimension of a doctrinal statement apparent, because, if it's in the gospel, it can only be liberating!

The subject of the quest for truth inevitably leads back to the question of the relationship between faith and reason. Can the gap that has opened up between the two be bridged?

It's vital that it should be, as much for faith as for reason. This is why John Paul II's encyclical, *Fides et Ratio*, is so important.[8] When we say Yes to God, we set out on a journey in the course of which our reason helps us to advance towards a glimpse of the mystery. So I truly believe that faith calls on reason. But, likewise, reason needs faith; otherwise, it lacks foundations.

You could put that another way: with the incarnation of his Son, God embraces all that is human, all that we are – our sense of beauty, our capacity for love, and, likewise, our ability to think. If Christ became human, then, in a certain way, our intelligence is blessed by God. We should make use of it. The nineteenth century was marked by an apparent conflict between scientists and theologians; between the microscope and the Bible. The former found new scientific explanations for the state of the world that appeared to contradict the Bible. This was an unnecessary battle, and the fruit of a mistaken and literalistic understanding of the Bible, and, thank God, it's largely over. I don't know any serious theologian who sees scientific statements as a threat to the faith. And most scientists have learned some humility. They know that their work rests on all sorts of acts of faith, on suppositions that they cannot prove.

10

Church and World

What can Christians contribute to today's world? How do you define the 'good news' they bring?

I could not claim to 'define' it, and certainly not in a few words. But I can say this: on the eve of his execution by the Nazis, on 9 April 1944, in Flossenburg concentration camp, that very great man, the Lutheran pastor Dietrich Bonhoeffer, sent to one of his English friends, the Anglican bishop of Chichester, George Bell, this message: 'The Victory is certain.'

Faced with the sufferings of humankind, with war, poverty and hatred, we too can say, 'The Victory is certain.' Faced with genocide in Rwanda, with the tragedies of the Balkans, when the defeat of humanity seems complete, we can say, 'The Victory is certain.' In the lives of each of us, even when our capacity for love and our courage seem destroyed, we can say, 'The Victory is certain.' When death takes someone we love and there seems to be no future, we discover that's not true. On Easter morning the disciples discovered that love had won over hate, friendship over betrayal, that sense had triumphed over non-sense, that the strong God makes us strong: 'The Victory is certain.' I once saw, in a church in Istanbul, a very fine fifteenth-century fresco showing the risen Christ breaking the chains of death and setting Adam and Eve free. Whatever the chains that bind us, the prisons that enclose us, we can rejoice and say, 'The Victory is certain.'

On the scale of the whole Church, what are, today, the main challenges to overcome if you are to proclaim this to the world?

The first challenge, in my view, is to find how to preach the gospel

to those who seem to have forgotten God, which is mainly a
phenomenon of the western world. We live in a culture saturated
with images: the press, posters, television, computers bombard us
with images that promise us life, excitement, happiness, achieve-
ment. When politicians are going through a difficult patch they
often say they have an 'image problem'. They then turn to a
specialist consultant who advises a new hairstyle, a new wardrobe
(my brethren cannot always resist dropping such hints to me!), who
advises them to be photographed on the football terraces or in the
pub . . . We have to admit that, today, the Church also has an 'image
problem'. It is seen as boring, moralizing and half-dead. But to put
this right we should not call in a consultant or try to 'reposition our
product' in the market. Christianity has nothing to do with that. At
the same time, are our hopes not focused on an image: that of
Christ: *imago Dei*, the image of God? The challenge facing
Christianity today is to make that image appear in all its beauty,
its vitality, its brilliance. Our streets are full of images – faces of pop
stars, film stars, footballers, politicians smiling, promising us the
earth. But these are only masks, and in the depths of our being we
are looking for an image that truly smiles on us, really sees us. The
Psalms are full of this longing, the desire to see the face of God:
'Your face, Lord, do I seek. Do not turn your face from me' (27:8–
9). We have to make this face visible, this icon of the living God
who Christ is.

One of the biggest struggles of the ancient Church was over
images of God. The Iconoclasts, who very nearly triumphed in the
Byzantine Church, claimed that these images should be forbidden.
Their defeat in the ninth century meant that, yes, it was possible to
show an image of God. This is what we need to rediscover today:
how to make that beauty visible. Through the liturgy, but also for
young people, in the streets, through dance, through music. . . .

Our second challenge is the remembrance of those who have
been forgotten. We live in a globalized world that puts us in touch
with ever more people. But, as the President of the United States
remarked recently, two-thirds of humanity live more than two
hours away from a telephone. Think of Africa, that magnificent
continent increasingly forgotten and invisible, crucified by violence,
by AIDS, by the resurgence of malaria. Never has so much money
been invested in medical research, but 90 per cent of the total is
devoted to the diseases of the rich. Even here, in the streets of

London, Paris or Rome, there are so many people we forget: the invisible poor, suffering from new forms of insecurity. If we want to proclaim the good news of the Kingdom in which the whole of humanity is made one, we must open our eyes to see the faces of our brothers and sisters who are becoming invisible. The final challenge, of which I have already spoken, is dialogue with those who have seen another face of God, members of other faiths. We should be attentive to them, learn from them, dialogue with them. Sometimes in the Church one may have the impression of a division between those who are in favour of the proclamation of the gospel and those who are in favour of dialogue. This is a false opposition: there is no preaching without dialogue. How can I preach without listening?

In fact, many Catholics see inter-faith dialogue as renouncing the commandment to 'make disciples of all nations'. How would you answer them?

If I preach the truth of Christ, I hope that will find an echo in the hearts and minds of my listeners. That may lead them into the Church or it may help them to find a new significance to their own religious tradition. In both cases, that is contributing to our pilgrimage towards unity.

What does 'making disciples' mean? It can sound like indoctrination. But the Greek word is *mathetes*, which means 'student'. A disciple, in the sense in which Christ used the term, is not someone who stops thinking. It is someone who is hungry to learn. Making disciples, it seems to me, is inviting people to search for the truth of God together. Some time ago, in Valencia in Spain, I met the Grand Rabbi and an important Muslim scholar to discuss setting up a Chair for the study of our three religions. What was wonderful about our discussions was that sharing what had the deepest meaning for each one of us made each of us disciples, students.

What should the Christian attitude to the world be? John Paul II recently told the German bishops, referring to John 15:19, 'You are not of the world, but don't cut yourselves off from the world.' How do you resolve this dilemma?

In my view, it's not a question of a dilemma but of a tension, and a necessary and fruitful one. As Christians, we proclaim Christ to be 'the light of the world'. It is in the light of Christ that we try to understand the contemporary world, to see it clearly, and also to criticize its values. At the same time, we are also people of this age, sharing the culture of our contemporaries. We read today's books, we see today's films. We share the tastes and prejudices, the strengths and the weaknesses of our time. We use the tools it offers us: psychology, sociology and anthropology can help us to understand the Word of God better. I find it encouraging that we are, at one and the same time, Christians who seek to understand the modern age, and contemporaries who seek to understand Christianity. There is a tension in this interaction, but it is a dynamic one. It is the Word of God becoming flesh in this world.

This tension is sometimes painful. . . .

Meister Eckhart[9] said that God is bringing the world to birth. Every birth is painful.

Isn't the Church often strongly tempted to withdraw from the world?

That temptation exists, it's true. But I think it's a temptation for the whole of western culture. From the start, even before the birth of Christianity, the west has always had an inclination to dualism: that is, to oppose soul and body, spirit and matter. It has always been tempted to seek salvation in rejection of the material world. This propensity also exists in some Asiatic cultures. I have the impression that one has to go to Africa and some American Indian societies to find cultures exempt from dualism. But at the very heart of Christianity there is the rejection of dualism. No other great religion attaches so much importance to the body. We state that our God took flesh, that he was born of a woman, like any child. The centre of our liturgy is the sharing of his body. The heart of our faith is the resurrection of the body. Christianity, in itself, is profoundly anti-dualist. From the start, Christianity opposed dualism. When St Paul preached the resurrection of the body, in Athens, people laughed at him. There was the battle against all forms of gnosticism, then against the great wave of Manicheism, which was deeply dualistic, in the fourth century. For a time St Augustine was a Manichean, and his difficulty, when he was coming close to Christianity, was precisely in accepting that the Word had become flesh. In the thirteenth century, it was Catharism to which Dominic was so intensely opposed.

Still today, contemporary thought is tempted by the duality of spirit and body. The English philosopher Mary Midgley wrote a fascinating study on the concept of salvation in modern science. She shows that many scientists believe that humanity will achieve perfection once it is liberated from the body. Look how seductive eastern spiritualities are, sometimes for the same reason. Christians living in this world cannot escape the attraction of dualism. But we have to go on fighting it and proclaiming that all that we are, the whole of our humanity, is saved.

To make the world understand it, should the Church come to terms with modernity and make its moral teaching fit contemporary behaviour, or should it go on resisting the evolution of the way we behave?

I think one must go back to that interaction of which I spoke of earlier. For example, the modern conception of relationship between the sexes has a lot to teach us, through the importance it attaches to intimacy, to equality in relationships, and so on. Modernity has helped us to open our eyes to aspects of scripture whose importance we may not have seen before. For example, now we see how extraordinarily free and open was Jesus' relationship with women. But at the same time, as Christians, we cast a critical eye over modernity in the light of the gospel. By and large, the contemporary sexual behaviour often degrades the profound beauty and significance of sexuality, trivializes it. I believe that, when all is said and done, the Church's teaching on sexuality is wise, good and liberating. We should not turn our backs on it. The challenge is to make people understand how this is so. We need to show that our teaching upholds the dignity of the person. We need to show that the Church's teaching is not based on the fear of sex but that it sees it as a gift of God, something much more beautiful and significant than the modern world imagines it to be.

Can such talk be understood by those who feel excluded by the Church's teaching – the divorced and remarried, homosexuals, those who have made use of abortion?

The Church, of its very nature, is inclusive of everyone. It is the sign of the unity of the whole human race and invites everyone into the Kingdom. It says, 'Come, enter into our Father's house.' Having said that, the path home will be different for different people. To vastly oversimplify, one can say that there are two types of reason why people find themselves in a situation of tension with the Church. The first concerns people whose ideas and attitudes are stamped with hatred. I am thinking of all forms of racism and prejudice, against blacks, against Jews, against homosexuals, and so on – all those ways of saying, 'That person is not my brother or sister.' In such cases, the Church's attitude should be completely unambiguous. We can meet people who propose such views, debate with them, try to convince them, but we must not say anything that allows them to think that their behaviour is even remotely compatible with the gospel. Hatred is fundamentally incompatible with the gospel.

Then there are others who have difficulties with the Church not because they hate but because they are living in a relationship that conflicts with the Church's teaching, such as unmarried couples, divorced and remarried couples, practising homosexuals, and so on. We should first of all recognize that at the heart of their relationship is love. Any love, as love, is good, is God's presence. The essential point of departure is their desire to love. We should recognize this and give it its value. The moral teaching of the Church should never consist in telling people that they should not love someone. It should only invite them to love better. There is no human love that is not in need of healing, which does not need to be led to maturity and fullness. That applies to married couples too. If we wish to show that the Church's moral teaching is good news, we have to be with people, enter their homes, enjoy their friendship. We have to understand how they see the world, learn what they have to teach us, see through their eyes, grow in mutual trust. Then we shall find how to express the Church's teaching, with them. God's friendship with the human race is the very heart of the gospel. So we cannot express our deepest moral convictions except in a context of friendship.

Couldn't the Church make this friendship dimension more obvious when it formulates its ex cathedra *pronouncements?*

One has to accept that any declaration by the Church which seems to question a way of life is resented as an attack, as almost intolerable. And we need to understand why. In Church circles I often hear it said that it is because people have lost the sense of sin. I am not at all convinced by this. Our society seems to me, on the contrary, to be haunted by an almost unbearable sense of guilt. People don't always have much idea of why they feel this culpability. Perhaps they are, in fact, idealistic, they may feel that they have failed those whom they love; their parents, their children or their spouse. Or perhaps it's because of the powerlessness we feel in the face of the poverty we see or in the world at large. If many people cannot cope with any mention of sin, is it because they don't believe in it or because they feel crushed by culpability? The first thing we have to do is to show that we are loved, in all our weakness. Unless there is this fundamental assurance, then it is hard to raise questions about any form of life.

I wish to add one thing: we live in a society that is searching for a morality. Positively, this can take the form of a real and fine commitment to mutual tolerance. Negatively it takes the form of accusation and indignation. Reading the British press, I am often struck by its strident indignation; people are denounced as evil in the name of morality. In such an atmosphere, it is not surprising that any pronouncement by the Church on moral issues is perceived as an accusation. That puts an enormous responsibility on the Church for how it expresses its teaching, but also an enormous responsibility on the media for how they give an account of it. If the Pope makes a speech about poverty and adds a sentence on contraception, it's just that one sentence that will be taken up by the press. The press often distorts Church teaching by presenting it within its own framework of accusation.

How do you explain that phenomenon?

You know, the gospel is very dangerous: it can change the face of the world. Gandhi said, 'Christianity is a wonderful thing, but it has never been tried!' One way of undermining the gospel's transforming power is to reduce the Church's teaching to just sexual morality. Then one can say that what one does in one's own bed is nobody else's concern. It's a way of trying to emasculate a message that, if we were to listen to it, could turn our lives upside down.

What do you mean by that?

We must go back once more to Christ's resurrection, which breaks through all limitations. We are hemmed in, impeded from full communion with other people by so many things: physical distance, but also difference of language, misunderstandings, lies, hostility and, above all, death. The night before he died, Jesus gathered together his friends to celebrate the Last Supper. At that meal we see both communion and all that destroys it. This was the meal of their love, but also of its failure. The disciples fled. They were overcome with fear. Judas sold him. Peter denied him. Christ was betrayed, suffered and died. Christ embraced in that Last Supper everything that could destroy communion. His resurrection was the triumph over all these limitations. His resurrection is pure communion, absolute unity, infinite transparency.

All human beings, deep down, aspire to this unlimited communion. We look for it in love. But in fact we can find it only fully in the resurrection, love's triumph. The gospel is the invitation to begin to live, here and now, this communion of the resurrection. With St Paul we proclaim the Christ who 'has broken down the dividing wall' (Ephesians 2:14), who calls us to break down the walls that divide us from each other. The gospel can break down the walls that separates Tutsis from Hutus, Serbs from Croats, Catholics from Protestants in Northern Ireland. It destroys the hatred in our hearts, the hostility within our families. It can transform those economic structures that make the rich ever richer and the poor ever poorer. Think of those extraordinary words of the Magnificat: 'He has brought down the powerful from their thrones, and lifted up the lowly; he has filled the hungry with good things, and sent the rich away empty' (Luke 1:52–3). It's a matter of much more than a political agenda: it's the resurrection breaking into our lives, here and now. And that can change our lives utterly. That is dangerous!

One of the phrases used to define the Church is Mater et magistra, *meaning that it is both mother and mistress – in the sense of teacher. How do you prevent the maternal aspect from being overlaid by the teaching?*

That's a vital question for someone whose title is *Magister*! The heart of the problem is the contemporary perception of what it means to teach. Since the Enlightenment, teaching – beginning with that of the Church – was often seen as threatening, those who teach as imposing their own convictions on others, requiring their submission, depriving them of the freedom to think for themselves. This is all part of that crisis of authority to which I devoted my contribution to the Synod on Europe.[10] All teaching seems suspect. Look at the way the word 'docile' has changed its meaning. Etymologically, it means 'teachable', and this is the meaning it had in the Middle Ages. Today, it evokes an attitude of submission. The traditional model of teaching in the Church, and especially the Order, had nothing to do with that. It sought to initiate people into discussion. The teacher was someone who instructed his students, but who also listened to them, who challenged them to answer him. The very essence of medieval teaching was the *quaestio disputata*, literally the 'question debated'. Subsequently, with the Enlightenment, there was a shift in the understanding of what it means to think, and it came to be seen as an essentially solitary act. Thinking meant going into one's room, closing the door and being on one's own, like Rodin's Thinker. This of course merely reflects the modern view of human beings; essentially alone, detached from others, as I pointed out earlier. This view is mistaken. We are not essentially solitary beings. We exist only in relationship to others, and this applies just as much to the activity of thinking. It is a social activity: we are initiated into discussion, learning to share ideas, to listen, to argue. Of course, from time to time we need to retire and reflect alone. But that's only one aspect of thinking, not the essence of it. To teach people how to think for themselves, you really have to teach them how to think with others. It's an initiation into the human community.

So one cannot oppose *mater* and *magistra*. In my view, teaching is a profoundly maternal activity. It is precisely the mother who introduces a child into the human community. With patient and attentive love, she teaches the child how to become human, how to belong. Can you imagine a more extraordinary act of teaching than that of a mother – or a father – helping an infant speak its first words? So in the Church there can be no fundamental opposition between the Church as *mater* and as *magistra*.

In the way it couches its teaching, has the Church taken sufficient account of
the development of the media? Formerly, when the Holy See issued a
doctrinal declaration, it did not come directly to the knowledge of the faithful.
They went first to the bishops, and then to the priests, who, in turn,
informed the faithful of it. This course allowed for some unpacking, an
inculturation in the local context. Today, when the Vatican publishes a text,
the media get hold of it immediately, and all the intermediary stages are
short-circuited. How would you see this new fact?

If we wish our teaching to be credible, in the first place we should
not be afraid of the Church being seen to be a community in which
there is debate, where we look for the truth together. We should
also not be afraid of sometimes saying that we don't have the
answer. Why did Cardinal Hume have such authority in England,
way beyond the Catholic world? Partly it was because when he
did not know the answer to a question, he had no hesitation in
saying so.

Also we have to build up a relationship of trust with those who
work in the media. We have to treat them as intelligent people;
work with them, take time to explain, to answer questions, to face
objections. This requires a real effort from of us, since we have to
overcome a reticence faced with the media. We often may feel that
the press so distorts, ridicules or renders the Church's teaching
banal, that we want to have nothing to do with it. That is an
understandable reaction, but we cannot afford to cut ourselves off.

Finally, we always need to ask ourselves how our teaching will be
understood. We need to put ourselves in the place of those who are
going to hear it. If we must express ourselves on contraception, we
need to try to imagine a couple's reaction. We need to use their
language as far as possible, to try to anticipate misunderstandings.
Often, the main problem with a teaching is not its content but the
language used to formulate it. I realize that this is immensely
difficult, when the Church's teaching is presented to the whole
world in a press release!

11

Reform

What reforms, in your opinion, are needed in the life of the Church?

In Vatican II's Decree on Ecumenism, *Unitatis redintegratio,* you find the words *Ecclesia semper reformanda:* the Church always being reformed. But the phrase is, in fact, much older; it goes back to the sixteenth century, to the time of the conflict with Lutheranism when the Church was forced to recognize that it needed reformation. So saying that the Church needs to be reformed is not disloyal. It is part of its pilgrimage. For the Church to be in need of reform is not a sign of failure; it means that it is alive, on its way to the Kingdom.

It seems to me that we are, first, in great need of renewal of the parish, especially in the west. Parishes often do not seem to be true communities imbued with God's joy and communion. How can we remedy that? I have to admit my incompetence here, having virtually no experience of parish ministry.

I also think that in many parts of the world we need to reflect upon the liturgy. This is one of the fundamental ways of showing God's beauty. Yet, all too often, the liturgy is boring. That's not true in Africa, India or some parts of Latin America, but in many places in Europe the liturgy seems dead.

Is that because of Vatican II's liturgical reform?

The liturgy of my childhood, before Vatican II, embodied a very strong sense of mystery and silence. But it did not always enrich one's mind, since everything was in Latin. You had mystery without understanding. The reform of the Council was right and needed. For the first time, you could hear the word of God in your own language, you could follow the words of the Eucharist prayer. We gained in understanding, but we lost the sense of mystery. We need both our heart and our mind to draw near to God. We have to discover how to celebrate the liturgy so that it is at once understandable, as it has been since Vatican II, and yet leads us to the mystery, as it did before Vatican II.

So should we reform the reform?

Why not? It takes centuries for the liturgy to evolve. It is not surprising if a mere 30 years after the Council we have not yet found how best to celebrate a new liturgy that is in the vernacular and yet truly beautiful. It takes time. In any case, I am convinced that nostalgia for the pre-Vatican is not helpful.

We are evoking Vatican II. How did you, personally, experience that event? And how do you explain that the interpretation of the Council still produces harsh debates among Catholics?

I joined the novitiate in September 1965, just three months before the closure of the Council. I told you earlier that I had never, until shortly before I joined the Order, been all that interested in my faith. I was extraordinarily ignorant. Before acceptance for the novitiate, there was an interview, and I remember a grave Dominican asking me, 'Which theologians have you read?' 'None,' I replied. 'Not even Schillebeeckx?' I had to confess that I had never heard of him. Fortunately, no one asked me to spell his name!

My theological awakening therefore happened in the climate of the post-conciliar Church. This meant that, in a way, I failed to appreciate the importance of Vatican II. It was as natural as the air one breathes. As young Dominicans, we grew up in that atmosphere of *Gaudium et spes*, of joy and hope – forgetting, of course, the words that come next, *luctus et angor*, grief and anxiety.[11] We had the feeling that the Church was at the start of an enormous transformation, and we instinctively looked more to the future than to the past, back to the Council. I remember a party in Paris, for Yves Congar's seventieth birthday. That was in 1974, just nine years after the Council. A friar made a speech in which he praised everything Congar had contributed to the Council. But then he added, 'Now, we're elsewhere' (*Maintenant nous sommes ailleurs*). For us, it was a time that was past.

Today, 35 years later, we are beginning to see the Council in perspective. It brought some magnificent and irreversible changes: liturgical reform, even if that still needs to be perfected; new relations with our sister Churches; a greater consciousness of the social implications of the gospel. How can we go back on all that?

It is true that there are arguments about Vatican II today, a tension between 'maximalist' and 'minimalist' interpretations of its teaching. But that's natural and inevitable. We shouldn't be afraid of debate! We should discuss the issues openly, clearly, listening to each other. Above all, don't let us stay in opposing camps bombarding each other from a distance, some claiming that the Council betrayed what was essential to the Church, and others claiming that now the Council is itself betrayed. All the major councils have been followed by years or decades of debate about their significance. Thirty years after Nicaea (325) it looked as though the Council had failed and Arianism had won the day. So, don't let's panic!

What are the points of Vatican II that you think are most in need of discussion?

Above all, matters relating to the government of the Church. Of all the Council's teachings, this is perhaps the one where we are furthest away from implementation. Vatican II insisted on the collegiality of bishops, on their shared responsibility for the government of the Church. On 15 September 1965, the very day after I joined the novitiate, Pope Paul VI promulgated the Apostolic Letter, *Apostolica sollicitudo*, fixing the rules for synods of bishops, which were to be bodies designed precisely to put this collegiality into effect. I am privileged to have been invited to take part in three synods; those devoted to religious life in 1994, to Oceania in 1998 and to Europe in 1999. These assemblies are useful, but they have not delivered all that one might have hoped of them: a real debate, a sharing of responsibility.

We need to go on looking for ways to assure the unity of the Church, centred on the successor of Peter while recognizing the role of bishops. John Paul II himself has encouraged us in this quest through his encyclical *Ut unum sint*,[12] in which he asked for advice on how his primacy should be exercised. We are still far from having answered him.

Would you go so far as to say that the Church is going through an institutional crisis?

I think it is. As an institution, the Church in many countries has lost authority and credibility. This is a fundamental challenge we have to face. Partly, this is a crisis of all institutions. All institutions have all become suspect – whether governments, the European Union, the United Nations, or whatever. This is partly linked to the contemporary conception of the human person. Today, as I have already said, we have a very individualistic, solitary conception of the person. And so any institution looks like a threat to our autonomy, our independence, our individual freedom. We need to rediscover that there can be no human life without institutions. We are not human except in relationship to other people. Today we recognize only the centrality of the couple. But human existence cannot rest on just this institution. We need multiple relationships: with friends, with colleagues, with people who share the same interests, who live in the same town, and so on. This means institutions: schools, courts, local government, police forces, even newspapers!

The Church is an institution and it has to be one. People often criticize the 'institutional Church', as if it were necessarily bad, in contrast to an unofficial 'Church of the people', which would be better. But the Church cannot be just a sort of movement, like the Israelites crossing the desert or a mob of football fans. We must have an institutional framework. The real question, then, is whether this works well. An institution is carrying out its function when it empowers all its members. Now it seems to me that this is not always the case in the Church. Lay people often complain that they are not being empowered by their priests, who complain of the same thing with regard to their bishops, who express the same complaint about the Vatican.

Part of the explanation, perhaps, lies in the fact that the Church's institutions have been over-simplified, the hierarchy of bishop–priest–deacon–lay person. Mary Douglas – who is both a Catholic and a very distinguished anthropologist – has shown that societies need various hierarchies, numerous institutions capable of sustaining different forms of life. This was previously the case in the Church in the Middle Ages, when the Church was made vital by many institutions: the religious Orders, the schools of theology, the guilds, and many other structures present in the life of society. Each of these institutions within the Church allowed people to have an identity and an authority. Nowadays, everything happens as though there were only 'the' hierarchy. But the solution does not lie in abolishing or weakening it; it's more a matter of strengthening or recognizing others.

Such as?

Cardinal Newman said there were three authorities in the Church: the authority of tradition, the authority of reason and the authority of experience, which he placed respectively in the hierarchy, the university and the body of the faithful. He added that if one of these three became too dominant, the right exercise of authority in the Church risked being compromised. Each needs to be strong; for example, the theological faculties have their authority. Charismatic movements, for example, easily tend to give too much authority to experience. There have been moments when reason appeared to be absolutized, as in some countries in eighteenth-century Europe. Today, I think that some groups within the Church give too exclusive a stress to tradition, to the detriment of reason and experience.

Is it time to begin to think of a new Council?

I think the challenge to bring out is rather to promote real and open discussion in the Church. We are too afraid of debate!

Why is that?

Because we fear that disagreement may be seen as a lack of unity. But this is not the case. There have always been disagreements in the life of the Church. Peter and Paul had passionate arguments about the nature of the Church. How can we overcome disagreement and reach consensus except through debate?

Where could such debates take place?

The synod of bishops could be one such place, more so than it is now, and also faculties of theology. Academics, you know, are just like everyone else; they are not exempt from the fear of real argument. This means that we often have 'progressive' and 'conservative' faculties, which gather together like-minded people, whereas we should have faculties of theology in which both sides can talk to each other, in the pursuit of truth.

If you go by views expressed in the papers, the most needed reforms would be in the areas of contraception, marriage discipline, priestly celibacy and women's ordination. Are these questions important in your view? Are they the key to Church renewal?

Once again, one must not put fundamental doctrines, such as the resurrection and divinity of Christ, on the same level as questions that are not of the same order. Our basic convictions are expressed above all in the Creed. Together with the sacraments they make up the core of our faith. All other aspects of teaching should be placed in relationship to them. Karl Rahner used to say that we should ask about every item of the Church's teaching what it taught us about Christ. In that sense, all these questions you mention are not crucial.

Nevertheless, these are questions that need to be taken very seriously because they are important to people. Contraception is undoubtedly not a fundamental question for our faith, but if it is important for a couple, then it is important for all of us. Priestly celibacy is not part of the Church's teaching: it is a discipline of the Latin tradition, and as such it is secondary. But if a priest wishes to marry, that is very important to him and so to us all. These questions are also important because they are symptomatic of a major challenge that we have already discussed, that of the interaction between Christianity and modernity.

Let's take the example of women. When the Church is discussed in the Anglo-Saxon press, it's often on this subject: the equality of women, their responsibility in the Church, their access or lack of it to the priesthood. These are important questions because women make up half of humanity – and certainly more than half of the Church! It's a debate that shows very clearly what happens when our ancient faith meets our modern world. The recognition of the dignity and full equality of women, their right to speak and to vote, is one of the most genuine achievements of the modern age, and we should be grateful for it. It poses a challenge to the Church, which is still an institution largely dominated by the men. We should accept that modernity has opened our eyes, and ask forgiveness for our mistakes in regard to women.

But our contemporaries are a little too ready to conclude, without hesitation, that women should be ordained. If women can be university professors, judges or prime minister, it seems obvious to our contemporaries that they should be priests. Well, it's not so obvious to me. Ordination is a sacrament, which means that it belongs to the order of the symbolic. Presiding at the Eucharist is, above all, a symbolic role and not a claim to status. Now, modernity is blind to the symbolic: it can conceive priesthood only in terms of power or status. The fact that almost all decisions in the Church are, in fact, in the hands of the clergy can, it is true, contribute to this misunderstanding. So we find ourselves in a situation where modernity is calling on the Church to recognize the equality of the sexes while the Church calls on modernity to recognize the profound importance of the symbolic.

Can a debate be prolonged to infinity? Doesn't a time come when it has to arrive at a decision?

The dynamic of debate consists in looking for a truth large enough to include what is true in both points of view. But sometimes a debate may fail to arrive at a consensus. Then the Church may have to make some authoritative declaration of its teaching and declare, 'This is what we believe'. This often happened in the early Church at Councils, after prolonged arguments about fundamental doctrines of our faith, belief in the divinity of Christ, the Trinity and so on. But this has the aim not so much of bringing all debate to an end – we shall never cease from exploration – as to move it to a new level, to get beyond an impasse. Earlier, I evoked the *quaestio disputata* of medieval universities. The moment came when the president of the session pronounced his *determinatio*.

If someone refuses to accept the determinatio, *should he be disciplined?*

Let us imagine that one of my Dominican brethren seems to deny the resurrection of Christ. The Order's reaction would be to open a dialogue with him. The first stage would consist in verifying whether he actually holds the position which is attributed to him. Very often, when a theologian finds a new way of expressing a truth, he is accused of denying it, while he is simply using terms to state it that we are not used to. To pursue the hypothesis: it appears, after this first stage, that this friar really is denying the resurrection. Is that the end? No, I need to understand why. Perhaps his position contains a right intuition that he has not succeeded in integrating into the Church's doctrinal framework. Perhaps he is opposed to this teaching because he has a mistaken understanding of it. Together, we need to examine how to resolve these difficulties, taking all the time needed, with no use of threats. But, you are going to ask me, what if, at the end of the day, that friar's position still cannot be reconciled with the Church's teaching? If we get to that point, then we have to be clear and face the consequences with him. But I can tell you that, after so many years of holding office in the Order, I have never yet reached that point.

12

End

To finish, can we come back to more personal questions? In the world of today, what gives you most cause for hope and what worries you most?

Are historical developments leading humanity closer to the perfect communion in the Kingdom or further away? We live at a time in history when the possibilities for communication between people are growing at an unheard-of rate. That is my hope. But there are also very strong forces threatening to destroy the human community. That is my worry.

Look at the extraordinary possibilities we now have for communicating with the whole world. Thanks to the Internet I can send a message to a friar who lives in the Antipodes. In a few seconds he will have it on his computer screen. Isn't that a wonderful tool for building up community? And yet more communication does not automatically imply greater communion. Surfing the net and sending e-mails does not always help us to escape the solitude of modern life. Those who spend most time in front of a computer or TV screen are often those who are alone, with no human face to smile at them in their own homes. In the western world, we may have more communication but the sense of local community has been dreadfully weakened. We don't even know the name of someone who lives on the same block, and is perhaps locked into the same solitude.

We live at a time when interdependence between all parts of the world is increasing. We exchange ever more products, films, books, ideas. Potentially, that is an enormous possibility of building our human community. But at the same time we are witnessing a terrible degradation of the quality of communication. Because the common denominator of much of this exchange has been reduced to money. The monetarization of all forms of human commerce over the past few centuries has reduced us to simple market functions. The English academic Nicholas Boyle has written that we all have a double identity: producer for the market and consumer in the market, with the mediating role between these two poles being money. The coins that bear Caesar's effigy may well triumph over human beings made in the image of God.

We live in a world in which rejection of war and longing for peace is strong. We have never been so convinced that violence solves nothing. We have never been so mobilized against poverty. Every major disaster provokes an international outburst of sympathy. We are witnessing the emergence of a universal human conscience. And yet we do not always face how we are implicated in this violence. Here in the western world we find it hard to admit that our countries have a responsibility for the perpetuation of wars and poverty – through our arms sales, through our trade and through our financial policies. Our opinion polls also show 'compassion fatigue': people cannot take any more images of suffering and violence on their TV screens. There is a great temptation to a new form of isolationism: switch off the television . . . and forget it.

Which forces are going to prove more powerful – those that strengthen community or those that erode it? I don't know. In the long term we know that communion will win: 'The victory is certain.' And in the short term I am optimistic – but maybe that's more because of my character than a rational position.

When you were elected Master of the Order, a British daily paper wrote of you: 'He has the capacity for associating the most progressive tolerance with the most conservative orthodoxy.' Does that strike you as accurate?

Not in the least. That sort of opposition is typical of a way of looking at the world that I absolutely do not share. First, I don't think I am really tolerant. Nor do I think that most progressives are: the most intolerant people I know are ideologues of left or right. Anyway, I don't think that a vague tolerance is always a good thing; in many ways it can be a paternalistic attitude that boils down to saying, 'You can think what you like.' But I do care what other people think. If I don't agree with them I want to tell them so. Of course, I try to respect their opinion, but that's something quite else.

I respect their opinion because I should never forget that perhaps it's *they* who are right, even if only partly so. If I find myself in disagreement with others, rather than just tolerating their opinion, I should try to find out how far I might be in the wrong.

Then, I do not agree with those who associate orthodoxy with a narrow conservatism, as if orthodoxy consisted in proclaiming a faith as unchanging as a mammoth trapped in ice. But that's not orthodoxy; it's actually a form of heresy. At the heart of orthodoxy there is a dynamic process pushing us towards the mystery, beyond our little beliefs, our little ideas. I am altogether for orthodoxy and I love the tradition. But the Church's tradition is complex, plural. It is so rich that most progress in the Church consists of rediscovering traditions that had been forgotten or neglected. The Reformation was a return to the Word of God; Vatican II drew on the treasure of the Church Fathers; Dominic invented a whole new form of religious Order, but in his eyes it was a return to the way that the apostles lived. That is to say that I am neither happy to be called a tolerant progressive nor an orthodox traditionalist. I am not fond of such labels!

What are you going to do when you come to the end of your term of office?

That's a pleasant question! Until now, I have not thought about it much, otherwise I should not be able to live in the present, tackle the questions that have to be dealt with today, respond to the brethren now. Whatever happens, I shall begin with a sabbatical period, which will be very unstructured. At present, I lead a fascinating but totally planned life: right now, I can tell you what I am going to be doing virtually every day for the next year or more. On my provincial visitations, my time is fixed hour by hour, perhaps over six weeks. So I look forward to that wonderful freedom of getting up in the morning not knowing what I will do that day.

And then? I trust in Providence. My life until now has been divided into periods of about twenty years, and I have never known what the next stage would be. For the first twenty years, I had no inkling that I was going to be a Dominican and a priest. Then, for the next twenty years, I studied and taught, thinking that would be my whole life. And I was very happy doing that. And then, while I was still teaching, I was elected prior. That began two decades of the

government in the Order. I am coming to the end of that stage, and
I have no idea what the next one will be. However, if I survive my
fourth twenty-year period, then I would rather like to end up in the
porter's lodge of a priory, answering the door and the phone. That
would satisfy my sociability and my insatiable curiosity!

If the Pope asked you to take charge of a diocese, would you accept?

That seems to me very unlikely. And it's not in the Order's
tradition.

There are some famous exceptions, including some today. . . .

That's true, but we have usually resisted. When St Albert the Great
was made a bishop, the Master of the Order, Humbert of Romans,
was furious and inveighed against the shame implied in a friar
renouncing poverty to put on the purple. Sometimes we must
accept, particularly in mission territory. Most Dominican bishops
have been missionary ones. Otherwise, it's not in our tradition, at
least unless there is a great deal of pressure put on us.

*You said at the beginning of the interviews that you had never stopped
believing in the existence of God. Have you really never doubted it?*

That question sounds a bit like, 'Have you never doubted the
existence of the Queen?' If I had such a doubt it could be resolved
by an invitation to Buckingham Palace. So one might imagine that
with God it would be enough to pop up to heaven to verify that
God is there. But to my mind that's too small a concept of God.
Saying that God exists is claiming far more than the existence of a
person I cannot see. It is proclaiming the existence of the One from
whom all things come and to whom all things return. Doubting the
existence of God means doubting that all that is has a meaning. Does
my life have a meaning? Do the existence of the world and the
history of the human race have meaning? That's the real question. I
don't remember ever having asked myself, 'Does God exist?' But
there may have been moments when I have asked, 'Does all this
make sense? Does my life make sense?'

It's never lasted long, but I have known such a moment of
darkness. In the history of the twentieth century, there was one

event that plunged us all collectively into this darkness, the Holocaust, that unspeakable horror of the deaths of millions of Jews, our cousins in faith. Faced with that, what can I say? Evil is a mystery, but I believe the mystery of God is greater.

In your letter to the brothers and sisters in the novitiate, [13] *you say that, before your solemn profession, you went through a 'long period of desolation.' Wasn't that a form of doubt?*

No, I did not doubt the existence of God or the meaning of my life. But God just seemed absent. There was no sense of the joy of God's presence with me. My belief was abstract, theoretical. I had not given up my commitment to my faith because I was convinced that this feeling of absence would eventually go away. I still had the joy of studying and the joy of friendship with the brethren, like pledges of the full joy I would surely find again. And that came, quite unexpectedly, in the Garden of Gethsemane, in Jerusalem. I was given that gift in just the right place, where Jesus knew the solitude of the deepest night, when he felt so distant from the Father. But there is no night, no solitude, no despair in which God has not been with Jesus and with everyone.

What happened in the Garden?

How can I put it? I didn't suddenly feel God's presence, like someone beside me. I think I rather rediscovered an inner depth in which 'God is closer to me than I am myself', in the words of St Augustine. Perhaps such experiences of absence are given to us just so that we can rediscover God deeper within us. Perhaps we have lost a certain conception of God, as a very affectionate invisible person, in order to rediscover God as the mystery that is at the heart of our existence and that gives us our existence at every moment.

What keeps your faith alive, what feeds it?

In the first place, living in a believing community. There may be a time when I have difficulty in my faith or in being sure of God's mercy. At such times, my brethren believe for me. Just as, at other times, it may be for me to believe for them. That's why we can truly say, 'We believe', and not 'I believe'.

There's something else that counts for much in our fraternal life, and that's listening to my brethren preach. Being a 'friar preacher' does not mean only that we are preachers but that we live in communities of preachers, that we listen to one another preach the Word of God. People in love need to hear their beloved saying 'I love you'. Those who are preachers also need to hear the simplest truths proclaimed to them, beginning with 'God loves you'. When I travel around the Order, Provincials often want me to preach non-stop. I have to insist that I need to listen to my brethren preaching and to receive the word of life from them. It's part of our brotherhood.

What feeds my faith is also seeing the joy of believers, the joy of some of our aged friars, the joy of our nuns and Sisters. That's when you really see that our faith is not a prison but a liberation.

Obviously, living with the word of God is fundamental. Meditating on scripture is almost like a daily meal at which you chew and then swallow the bread of the Word of God. What is extraordinary is that it's possible to have lived for more than 30 years as a Dominican and still be surprised by scripture. That came to me quite recently when I was reading the book of *Job*, that man who felt himself reaching the limits of despair. I then realized how true it is that there's no doubt, no distress that does not have a place in scripture, and that does not find an answer there.

How do you face death?

So far, I have never felt afraid of death, my own death. Belief in the resurrection is central to my faith. Also I have been helped to face death by being with many of my brethren at the time of their deaths, and seen them face death calmly, with serenity. Our tradition is to sing the *Salve Regina* with the brethren as they face death, and that is beautiful. Sometimes the way a brother dies is his last gift to the community, his last preaching of the gospel, which gives us all hope. So far, I have never had to really face my own mortality, and so, perhaps, when the time comes I will be not nearly as calm and trusting as I hope! But I trust that my brethren will help me then. But also, dying is not just an event at the end. We practise it all the time, every time we try to break through the barriers of our egotism and let God's grace change us. One of my brethren said the other day, 'He who has never done anything new will have a hard time dying.'

How do you pray? How do you dialogue with God?

In the Dominican tradition, prayer is often regarded as an act of friendship. We talk to God as to a friend. As there are no techniques for friendship, we really have no technique of prayer. I have to admit that I'm not very good at praying; I get distracted very easily. I often go into the chapel, just to sit down and spend some time with God, in silence. But often my head and my heart are too busy for that. I am too caught up in my problems, letters waiting on my desk, often too concerned with myself. One day, Noel Coward met a friend of his at a party and said to him, 'We haven't time to talk about both of us, so let's talk about me.' Our prayer often is a little like that. We address God lots of worthy words, while we're really thinking about ourselves and what there is to dinner. But if you give yourself enough time, the moment of silence comes when one is simply alone with God. Prayer is not thinking about God. As my fellow novice Simon Tugwell said, when we are with our friends we don't think about them; we are just with them. Prayer is putting ourselves in God's presence.

Sometimes, I take a verse from scripture. I read it, meditate on it, let it penetrate me. I repeat it until it breaks down the barriers of my selfishness, opens me up. At present, it's this line from Psalm 143: 'In the morning, let me know your love.' If we could really know this love, even a little more, would not everything be changed? But at the same time, allowing myself to be seized by this love means accepting a radical transformation of myself. It means abandoning my armour, my hardness, and setting out on a journey that will break my heart of stone, which is rather frightening, and painful. St Augustine said in his prayer: 'Lord, make me chaste, but not yet.' I sometimes catch myself praying in the same way: 'Lord, make me holy, transform me, but not just yet, not before I have finished my term as Master, not before I've settled this problem, not until the spring . . .' I hope that one day I shall stop saying, 'Not just yet'. Till then, God waits patiently, like a friend.

1 The convent on the Aventine Hill in Rome, where the administrative headquarters of the Order are located.

2   The operation was called off at the last minute, after mediation by the UN Secretary General, Kofi Annan.
3   In *Sing a New Song* (Dominican Publications, Dublin), 1999, pp. 121–59.
4   Master of the Order from 1222 to 1237.
5   Dominican nun, lived 1201–36.
6   Congar: 1904–95; Chenu: 1895–1990; Schillebeeckx: 1914–.
7   Founded by the Dominicans in 1580, the Angelicum is one of the five pontifical universities of Rome. The Master of the Order is, by statute, its Chancellor.
8   Published in October 1998.
9   German Dominican theologian, ?1260–?1327.
10 See pages 135–7.
11 The Pastoral Constitution Gaudium et spes, on the Church in the Modern World (7 December 1965), is one of the most important documents of the Council. It begins with these words: 'The joys and the hopes, the griefs and the anxieties of the [people] of this age, especially those who are poor or in any way afflicted, these too are the joys and hopes, the griefs and anxieties of the followers of Christ. Indeed, nothing genuinely human fails to raise an echo in their hearts.'
12 Encyclical on ecumenical involvement, published in May 1995.
13 In *Sing a New Song* (Dominican Publications, Dublin), 1999, pp. 160-8.

Part Two

Christian Commitment

Making Promises till Death[1]

At the Last Supper Peter makes a rash promise to Jesus: 'I will lay down my life for you.' In one way it is not a good model for how to make vows. There is no evidence of a deliberate and mature decision. A promise to marry someone made as impulsively as that could easily be annulled. Nevertheless Peter's vow offers hope to us who make vows. It suggests why we may dare to promise fidelity to anyone, our husband or wife or God.

In our society, the making of vows has no great credibility. When one in three marriages ends in divorce and a recent book, *Shattered Vows*, maintains that priests and religious are giving up their vows in droves, then can we take these promises seriously? As Glynn de Moss said when he married for the twenty-second time, 'Divorce does not upset me. It's another racoon skin on the wall.' Should we carry on even pretending? Peter's vow suggests why we may dare to do such a thing.

Peter says to Jesus, 'I will lay down my life for you.' And according to St John, Jesus replied, 'You will lay down your life for me. But truly, truly I say to you, the cock will not crow till you have denied me three times.' So Peter makes a mad promise and within hours he has broken it. But in the end God opens up a way for him beyond failure.

Peter warms himself at the charcoal fire in the palace of the high priest and three times he denies Christ. Then in the last chapter, we find him once again at a charcoal fire on the seashore, undoing the denial. Three times Jesus asks him, 'Peter do you love me?' And three times Peter unknits his failure and confesses that he does. Then Jesus picks up the rash promise of the Last Supper and binds Peter to it:

'Truly, Truly. I say to you, when you were young, you girded yourself
and walked where you would; but when you are old, you will stretch
out your hands and another will gird you and carry you where you do
not wish to go.' [This he said to show by what death he was to give glory
to God.]

Peter's words stand.

Human dignity

Nothing that I write is intended to be the slightest judgement on
those whose vows have collapsed, whose marriages have failed or
who given up their religious vocations. It is not for us to make a
judgement. Maybe it is simply a fact that sometimes vows become
impossible to sustain. We must be honest. All that I wish to do is to
suggest why, even in a society which tends not to take promises very
seriously, they are fundamental to human dignity and why we may
dare to risk so binding ourselves.

The first reason why we should make vows is because God does.
The story of our salvation is of the God who revealed himself to us
as the one who makes covenants. After the Flood he came to Noah
and promised that never again would the earth be covered with
water and humanity destroyed. He vowed to bless Abraham. He
appeared to Moses and told him his name, I AM, and he promised
that he would bring his people out of affliction in Egypt.

Making promises is not just something that God happens to do. It
discloses who he is. I AM will deliver you. And we see the fullness
of who he is in Jesus, in whom all the promises are fulfilled.

So the first reason why we should have the confidence to dare to
make promises – perhaps not quite as impulsively as Peter unless you
want a get-out clause later on – is because we are God's children. It
is part of our dignity that we can do this thing. Cats and dogs can be
loyal and faithful, but they cannot make promises. We show God to
the world by daring to follow our Father's example. One of the
ways in which society can subvert our dignity, is by undermining
the vows that we make.

When the British brought slaves to work on the plantations in the
West Indies, we systematically tried to break down their marriages.
We broke up couples, forbade marriage ceremonies, dispersed
families. And that meant that we were attacking the slaves at their

deepest level, as people who were like God and made promises. But the slaves refused to accept this humiliation. They stuck to their dignity. They invented their own ceremonies. They showed that whatever the white plantation owners might think, they were the children of God and made in his image. Our own society does this more subtly through the pressures of work and the presentation of marriage and sexuality in the media. Elton John's 'Everyone needs a part-time lover' does not exactly conjure up the fidelity of the God of Abraham, Isaac and Jacob!

Anyone who makes a vow can soon find themselves in Peter's situation. Classically it is almost immediately after people have got married or ordained that they often find themselves in a mess. One might call it the Petrine syndrome. According to St John the guards come and arrest Jesus. 'Whom do you seek?,' he asks. 'Jesus of Nazareth.' And Jesus replies 'I am'. He is not just saying that he is the person for whom they are looking. Twice he uses the divine name, I AM. Here is the revelation of the God of Moses who promised to bring the people out from the affliction of Egypt. And when the maid-servant comes and asks Peter whether he is not one of Jesus' disciples, then twice he says, 'I am not'. He denies that he is a child of the God of promises. Also he denies himself. He rejects his own identity. At the charcoal fire on the beach, three times he can claim back that identity, 'You know that I love you'. It is not just that he is forgiven. He has become himself again.

The future

One reason why our society tends not to take promises very seriously is that it finds it hard to believe that vows touch our identity so very profoundly. I remember a foreign Provincial telling me that one day he talked with a student in simple vows who was just coming up to solemn profession and so he asked him, 'Can you really promise to be faithful till death?' And the student said:

> 'It depends upon what you mean. If you mean: Will I be faithful no matter what you ask of me, even if it demands my life? then the answer is: Yes. But if you mean: will I go on being a Dominican until the day that I die? Well, I do not know. Who knows who I will become?'

It is one thing to say that one will give everything, offer all that one is now, and it is another to promise to go on year after year, no matter what happens, and whom one meets and with whom one may fall in love. It is the same doubt that hits people when they are faced with promising to marry. To love someone is almost by definition to offer them all that you have and are. But the one thing that people can find hard to promise is the future; we can promise all except time, all of our time. Why is this form of commitment so hard to make?

In part it is that unlike our ancestors, we probably feel that we change as we grow older, we are not the same person. How can I bind someone who is not yet, who does not yet exist, the person I will be?

If ever you have to see and counsel people whose marriages are on the rocks, or the brethren or sisters in tough times, they may say something like this:

> 'I am not the same person as the one who married Jane or Edward, or who made solemn profession or promised obedience to his bishop. Then I was young and naïve; since then I have travelled, I have discovered Mozart and Madonna, had experience, got degrees. I am not the same person as that young idealistic, bright eyed twenty-five year old. I cannot be bound by the promises that that person made. That person does not exist anymore.'

In the words of Donne, 'We are not just those persons, which we were'.

The making of vows only has any meaning if one believes that the person who made that promise persists. Who I am is not to be known in a moment but discovered in the story of my whole life. Promises for the *Now Generation* are a celebration of a *depth* of commitment rather than its *extension* through time. Our sense of who we are, of what it means for me to be me, tends to be just rooted in this moment, with its pleasures and its crises.

Alasdair McIntyre wrote:

> Modernity partitions each human life into a variety of segments, each with its own norms and modes of behaviour. So work is divided from leisure, private life from public, the corporate from the personal. So both childhood and old age have been wrenched away from the rest of human life and made over into distinct realms. And all these separations have been achieved so that it is the distinctiveness of each and not the unity of the life of the individual who passes through those parts in terms of which we are taught to think.

There are magazines for children, TV programmes for the over 80s, holidays for young single people. There is a whole new type of TV programme in the United States, which is about the love-lives of people in their forties. So all the time we are being encouraged not to think of ourselves as people whose lives only make sense as a whole, but as people of just this moment, this time, this age. And that means that when our lives do not seem to make sense, when we have some sort of crisis, it will seem unsurpassable for this moment is the only one I have got! For the *Now Generation* a crisis now is a crisis without possible relief.

Longer story

What the story of Peter offers us is a longer story, that goes from his calling at Galilee, his journey to Jerusalem with Jesus, uncertain and afraid, through betrayal, to the meeting on the seashore where all is healed. It is only as we find ourselves in that longer story that vows can make sense, that we can cope with the failures and not be crushed by them and find ourselves carried beyond them. It is this longer sense of time, from birth to death and ultimately from Creation to Kingdom, that can make sense of anything so rash as saying 'I promise'. It is the longer story that we remember in the annual repetition of the liturgical year which carries us beyond the garden of Gethsemane, beyond Good Friday, to Easter and another charcoal fire.

While one is still on the journey, often it will be impossible to understand the meaning of one's vows. At the Last Supper Peter said to Jesus, 'Where are you going?' Jesus answered, 'Where I am going you cannot follow me now; but you shall follow afterwards.' Peter said to him, 'Lord, why cannot I follow you now? I will lay down my life for you.'

'Where are you going?' Peter vows to follow Jesus although he does not know to where. Like Pilate he does not wait for an answer. He cannot know what his vow means. The question remains unanswered almost until the end. There is a second-century legend that one day, during the persecutions, Peter was fleeing from Rome to save his life, when he met Jesus walking in the opposite direction. And once again, a second time, he said to Jesus, 'Where are you going? *Quo vadis?*' And Jesus said, 'I am going to Rome to die.' So Peter turned around and, at last, fulfilled his promise to Christ. Only at the end does he have an answer to his question.

Whenever we make promises, in baptism, marriage or religious life, we cannot know where they will land us. Every vow has its implicit and unanswered question, *Quo vadis?* We cannot imagine what it will mean to be married to this person, who may turn out to be sick, alcoholic or plain nasty. We cannot envisage what it will mean to pledge yourself to an Order that may send you to Iceland or ask you to learn Chinese, or just leave you without support or friendship. It is of the nature of a vow that it is yoked to Peter's unanswered question.

Hanging in

It will surely be the case that everyone who makes a promise will some time feel that it is futile to try to keep it. What possible sense could there be in remaining married to this man? Is there any sense in carrying on as a priest when life with Edwina would be so much more satisfying? We could even raise a good Catholic family and do our bit for the Church that way. Maybe one has a moral obligation to leave! But we may have to witness to the God who makes promises by hanging in there, as he hung on the cross.

In our lives we will see people to whom there is almost nothing that we can say; people who have lost a wife or husband, suffered breakdown; people in poverty, who have dropped out of society and can find no way back; people at the door asking for food and a bit of hope. What can we say? What possible sense can we make of their experience? Sometimes all that we can tell them about is the God who has made promises, to heal us, to raise us from the dead, and to bring the Kingdom. And how can we talk of the God who makes promises unless there is a sign? And the sign is the wife and husband pledging their word; the young monk or nun or sister or friar making a promise. Or there is the single person keeping faith with God, abiding by the vows of baptism, or keeping faithful to whatever promises they have made. In a society in which millions of people have no grounds for hope, no prospect of getting a job, resigned to lifelong unemployment, then the God of promises is sometimes the only God we can preach.

Promise to be poor

Recently I visited a community of the Little Sisters of Charles de Foucauld, living in a *barrio* on the edge of Lisbon near the airport. The people living there were mainly African immigrants, from Mozambique, Guinea and Angola, and a few gypsies, without water or electricity, and threatened with eviction. When I arrived the floor was covered with children making paintings, because the next week there was to be a feast. One of the sisters was to make her solemn profession. Everyone was involved in the preparation for the Mass and the meal. On the day a thousand people came, crammed into the shed they had borrowed for the occasion. It was their day, when Portuguese and Africans and gypsies could dance and sing together. And why did they all celebrate, the ones with faith and the ones who were not quite sure? Because if she would come and share their life, and make a promise to be poor with them, then there must be hope. This surely was an occasion which disclosed what it meant to make a promise.

Once the Master of the Dominican Order went to receive the solemn professions of three young friars who were in prison in Brazil. An entire community had been arrested as part of a persecution of the Order by the then military government, because of their witness to human rights. They were falsely accused of supporting a communist plot. It was an unusual place for friars to make their vows, but perhaps it disclosed what all vowing is about, confidence in the God who is faithful to us, who has promised that just world which is the Kingdom, and who will be faithful to his promise.

The Hebrew word for 'to promise' is *dabar*, to speak a word. The God who promises is simply the God who gives a word. And so what is at issue is simply: Do our words matter? Do our words have weight?

God's providence

This may sound a grim vision of fidelity. Having made a vow one has simply to endure until the end. One is stuck with one's husband or wife or life as a religious, and there is no imaginable future except hanging on. Could God possibly ask that? And if we are honest, sometimes that seems hard to believe. Some marriages do collapse and there seems to be no way forward. But implicitly we can only take vows trusting in God's providence. The God of promises will provide. When God tells Abraham to take his son Isaac to offer him as a sacrifice on the mountain, then God provides the lamb. 'On the mountain, the Lord will provide.' So a vow is not a statement of confidence in our strength but of hope in God's providence. Peter is weak and he does fail, but it is Jesus who opens out a way beyond. The rash promise of Peter undermines any vision of our vows as based on strength of will. Peter chooses the charcoal fire in the palace of the high priest but God provides the charcoal fire on the seashore. For some people nothing does seem to be provided, and I can only ask forgiveness for not reflecting on their experience. One cannot do everything.

One final point: Peter's vow is a vow to die. 'I will lay down my life for you.' The vows that shape our lives, that give them coherence and a pattern rather than just a succession of moments, are all made in the face of death. In our baptismal vows we are joined to the death of Christ, in marriage we are vowed 'until death us do part', and religious vows are *usque ad mortem*, until death. Vows confront us with our own mortality. Perhaps one of the reasons why we today find it so hard to embrace vows is because we flee the fact that we must die. Our society is founded on the dream of control, of the environment, of each other, but death shows us the limits of our power. We can put someone on the moon, but we must still die.

In *A Single Man*, a novel by Christopher Isherwood, a middle-aged man looks at himself in a mirror:

> Staring and staring into the mirror it sees many faces within its face – the face of the child, the boy, the young man, the not-so-young man – all present still, preserved like fossils on the superimposed layers, and, like fossils, dead. Their message to this live, dying creature is: Look at us – we have died – what is there to be afraid of? It answers them: But it happened so gradually, so easily. I'm afraid of being rushed.

'I am afraid of being rushed.' But we do not take vows alone. We take vows to and with each other. Vows are with and in a community. And perhaps we can only dare to make them because the community, our friends and brothers and sisters, help us to face and embrace our mortality. We can dare to let go.

Every act of making vows is an act of trust. There is always that unanswered question of Peter. 'But where, Lord, are you going?', most acutely when one faces death. One places oneself in the hands of God, but in the words of D. H. Lawrence, 'It is a fearful thing to fall into the hands of the living God. But it is a far more fearful thing to fall out of them.'

1   An article in *Priest and People*, July 1989, pp. 259–63.

The Throne of God

Note: A lecture given to the World Congress of Benedictine Abbots in Rome, September 2000.

It is a great honour for me to be asked to speak to this Congress of Abbots. I want to say a little about the role of monasteries in the new millennium. I feel so little suited to speak about this that I wonder whether I ought to have accepted the invitation. I did so just as an act of gratitude to St Benedict and those who follow his rule. I was educated – more or less – by the Benedictines for ten years, at Worth and Downside Abbeys, and I have the happiest memories of those years. Above all I remember the humanity of the monks, who helped me to believe in a God who was good and merciful, though very English! I probably owe my religious vocation to a great uncle who was a Benedictine, Dom John Lane Fox, whose vitality and enthusiasm for God was a great gift. And finally, I would like to thank God for that good Benedictine and friend, Cardinal Basil Hume.

Benedictine abbeys have been like oases in the pilgrimage of my life, where I have been able to rest and be refreshed before carrying on the journey. I did my diaconate retreat in Buckfast Abbey, and my retreat before ordination to the priesthood in Bec-Hellouin in Normandy. I spent holidays at *La Pierre qui vire*, and Einsideln, and celebrated Easter at Pannenhalme in Hungary, visited Subiaco, Monte Casino, Monte Olivetti and 100 more abbeys.

Everywhere I have gone, I have found crowds of people who were visiting the monasteries. Why are they there? Some, no doubt, are tourists who have come to pass an afternoon perhaps hoping to see a monk, like a monkey in a zoo. We might expect to find notices that say 'Do not feed the monks'. Others come for the beauty of the buildings or the liturgy. Many come hoping for some encounter with God. We talk about 'secularization', but we live in a time marked by a deep religious search. There is a hunger for the transcendent. People look for it in eastern religious, in new-age sects, in the exotic and the esoteric. Often there is a suspicion of the Church and all institutional religion, except perhaps for the monasteries. Still there is a trust that in the monasteries we may glimpse the mystery of God, and discover some hint of the transcendent.

Indeed, it is the role of the monastery to welcome these strangers. The Rule tells us that the stranger must be welcomed like Christ. He must be greeted with reverence, his feet must be washed and he must be fed. This has always been my experience. I remember going to visit St Otilien, when Bishop Viktor Dammertz was Abbot. I was a poor, dirty, hitch-hiking English Dominican student, and I was taken in by these very clean German Benedictines. I was washed, scrubbed and my hair was cut. I was almost respectable when I left to take to the road again. It did not last for long!

Why are people so drawn to monasteries? Today I would like to share with you some thoughts as to why this is so. You may think that my thoughts are completely crazy, and proof that a Dominican can understand nothing of the Benedictine life. If so, then please forgive me. I wish to claim that your monasteries disclose God not because of what you do or say, but perhaps because the monastic life has, at its centre, a space, a void in which God may show Himself. I wish to suggest that the rule of St Benedict offers a sort of hollow centre to your lives, in which God may live and be glimpsed.

The glory of God always shows itself in an empty space. When the Israelites came out of the desert, God came with them seated in the space between the wings of the cherubim, above the seat of mercy. The throne of glory was this void. It was only a small space, a hand's breadth. God does not need much space to show his glory. Down the Aventine, not 200 metres away, is the Basilica of Santa Sabina. And on its door is the first known representation of the cross. Here we see a throne of glory which is also a void, an absence, as a man dies crying out for the God who seems to have deserted him. The ultimate throne of glory is an empty tomb, where there is no body.

My hope is that Benedictine monasteries will continue to be places in which the glory of God shines out, thrones for the mystery.

And this is because of what you are not, and what you do not do. In recent years astronomers have been searching the skies for new planets. Until recently they could never see any planets directly. But they could detect them by a wobble in the orbit of the star. Perhaps with those who follow the rule of St Benedict it is similar, only you are the planets which disclose the invisible star which is the centre of the monastery. The measured orbit of your life points to the mystery which we cannot see directly. 'Truly, you are a hidden God, O God of Israel' (Isaiah 45:13).

I would like to suggest then that the invisible centre of your life is revealed in how you live. The glory of God is shown in a void, an empty space in your lives. I will suggest three aspects of the monastic life which open this void and make a space for God. First of all, your lives are for no particular purpose. Secondly, in that they lead nowhere, and finally because they are lives of humility. Each of these aspects of the monastic life opens us a space for God. And I wish to suggest that in each case it is the celebration of the liturgy that makes sense of this void. It is the singing of the Office several times a day that shows that this void is filled with the glory of God.

Being there

The most obvious fact about monks is that you do not do anything in particular. You farm but you are not farmers. You teach, but you are not schoolteachers. You may even run hospitals, or mission stations, but you are not primarily doctors or missionaries. You are monks, who follow the rule of Benedict. You do not do anything in particular. Monks are usually very busy people but the business is not the point and purpose of your lives. Cardinal Hume once wrote that

> we do not see ourselves as having any particular mission or function in the Church. We do not set out to change the course of history. We are just there almost by accident from a human point of view. And, happily, we go on 'just being there'.[1]

It is this absence of explicit purpose that discloses God as the secret, hidden purpose of your lives. God is disclosed as the invisible centre of our lives when we do not try to give any other justification for who we are. The point of the Christian life is just to be with God. Jesus says to the disciples: 'Abide in my love' (John 15:10).

Monks are called to abide in his love.

Our world is a market-place. Everyone is competing for attention, and trying to convince others that what they sell is necessary for the good life. All the time we are being told what we need so as to be happy: a microwave, a computer, a holiday in the Caribbean, a new soap. And it is tempting for religion to come to the market-place and to try to shout along with the other competitors. 'You need religion to be happy, to be successful and even to be rich.' One of the reasons for the explosion of the sects in Latin America is that they promise wealth. And so Christianity is there, proclaiming that it is relevant to your life. Yoga this week, aromatherapy next week. Can we persuade them to give Christianity a try? I remember a lavatory in a pub in Oxford. There was a graffito written in tiny letters, in a corner of the ceiling. And it said: 'If you have looked this far then you must be looking for something. Why not try the Roman Catholic Church?'

We need Christians out there, shouting along with the rest, joining in the bustle of the market-place, trying to catch people's eyes. That is where Dominicans and Franciscans, for example, should be. But the monasteries embody a deep truth. Ultimately, we worship God, not because he is relevant for us but simply because he is. The voice from the burning bush proclaimed 'I am who I am'. What matters is not that God is relevant to us, but that in God we find the disclosure of all relevance, the lodestar of our lives. I think that this was the secret of Cardinal Hume's unique authority. He did not try to market religion, and show that Catholicism was the secret ingredient for the successful life. He was just a monk who said his prayers. Deep down, people know that a God who must show that he is useful for me is not worth worshipping. A God who has to be relevant is not God at all. The life of the monk witnesses to the irrelevance of God, for everything is only relevant *in relation* to God. The lives of monks bear witness to that, by not doing anything in particular, except to abide with God. Your lives have a void at their centres, like the space between the wings of the cherubim. Here we may glimpse God's glory.

Perhaps the role of the Abbot is to be the person who obviously does nothing in particular. Other monks may get caught up in being bursar, or infirmarian, or running the farm or the printing house, or the school. But perhaps I can be so bold as to suggest that the Abbot might be the person who is guardian of the monks' deepest identity as those who have nothing in particular to do. There was an English Dominican called Bede Jarret, who was Provincial for many years: a famous preacher, a prolific writer of books. But he never appeared to do anything. If you went to see him, then I am told that he was usually doing nothing. If you asked him what he was doing, then I am told that he usually replied, 'Waiting to see if anyone came.' He perfected the art of doing much while appearing to do little. Most of us, including myself, do the opposite; we ensure that we always appear to be extremely busy, even when there is nothing to do!

When people flock to the monasteries, and look at the monks, and stay to hear Vespers, then how may they discover that this nothingness is a revelation of God? Why do they not just think of monks as people who are either lazy or without ambition; uncompetitive failures in the rat race of life? How may they glimpse that it is God who is at the centre of your lives? I suspect that it is by listening to your singing. The authority for that summons is found in the beauty of your praise of God. Lives that have no especial purpose are indeed a puzzle and a question. 'Why are these monks here and for what? What is their purpose?' It is the beauty of the praise of God that shows why you are here. When I was a young boy at Downside Abbey, I must confess that I was not very religious. I smoked behind the classrooms, and escaped at night to the pubs. I was almost expelled from school for reading a notorious book, *Lady Chatterley's Lover*, during benediction. If one thing kept me anchored in my faith, then it was the beauty that I found there: the beauty of the sung Office, the luminosity of the early morning in the Abbey, the radiance of the silence. It was the beauty that would not let me go.

It is surely no coincidence that the great theologian of beauty, Hans Ulrich von Balthasar, received his earliest education at Engelberg, a Benedictine school famous for its musical tradition. Balthasar talks of the 'self-evidence' of beauty, 'its intrinsic authority'.[2] You cannot argue with beauty's summons or dismiss it. And this is probably the most resounding form of God's authority in this age, in which art has become a form of religion. Few people may go to church on a Sunday, but millions go to concerts and art galleries and museums. In beauty we can glimpse the glory of God's wisdom which danced when she made the world, 'more beautiful than the sun' (Wisdom 7). In the Septuagint, the early Greek translation of the Bible, when God made the world, then he saw that it was *kala*, beautiful. Goodness summons us in the form of beauty. When people hear the beauty of the singing, then they may indeed guess why the monks are there and what is the secret centre of their lives, the praise of glory. It was typical of Dom Basil that when he talked about the deepest desires of his heart, then he talked in terms of beauty:

> What an experience it would be if I could know that which among the most beautiful things was the most beautiful of them all. That would be the highest of all the experiences of joy, and total fulfilment. The most beautiful of all things I call God.[3]

And if beauty is truly the revelation of the good and the true, as St Thomas Aquinas believed, then perhaps part of the vocation of the Church is to be a place of the revelation of true beauty. Much modern music, even in Church, is so trivial that it is a parody of beauty. It is kitsch which has been described as the 'pornography of insignificance'.[4] Maybe it is because we fall into the trap of seeing beauty in utilitarian terms, useful for entertaining people, instead of seeing that what is truly beautiful reveals the good.

I hope that you will not think it too bizarre if I say that I believe that the monastic way of life is in itself beautiful. I was fascinated when I read the Rule to see that it says at the beginning that 'It is called a rule because it regulates the lives of those who obey it.' The *regula* regulates. At first that sounds all too controlling for a Dominican. In my experience, it is very hard to regulate the friars! But perhaps *regula* suggests not control so much as measure, rhythm, lives which have a shape and a form. Perhaps what it suggests is the discipline of music. St Augustine thought that to live virtuously was to live musically, to be in harmony. Loving one's neighbour was, he said, 'keeping musical order'.[5] Grace is graceful and the graced life is beautiful.

So once again it is the singing of the liturgy that discloses the meaning of our lives. St Thomas said that beauty in music was essentially linked to *temperantia*. Nothing should ever be in excess. Music must keep the right beat, neither too fast nor too slow, keeping the right measure. And Thomas thought that the temperate life kept us young and beautiful. But what the Rule appears to offer is especially a measured life, with nothing in excess, though I do not know whether monks stay any younger and more beautiful than anyone else! The Rule admits that in the past monks did not drink at all, but since we cannot convince monks not to drink, then at least it must be in moderation. Nothing to excess.

I am reminded of my Benedictine great-uncle who had a great love of wine, which he was sure was necessary for his health. Since he lived to be almost 100, then perhaps he was right. He persuaded my father and uncles to keep him well supplied with a daily bottle of claret, which I suppose could be called moderate, and, in accordance with the Rule, a *hemina* (Chapter 40). When he smuggled these back into the monastery, the monks always wondered what caused the clinking noises in his bag. Elaborate explanations were prepared in advance with the help of his nephews!

When we hear monks sing, we glimpse the music that is your lives, following the rhythm and beat of the tune of the Rule of St Benedict. The glory of God is enthroned on the praises of Israel.

Going nowhere

The lives of monks puzzle the outsider not just because you do not do anything in particular, but also because your lives go nowhere. Like all members of religious orders, your lives do not have shape and meaning through climbing a ladder of promotion. We are just brethren and sisters, friars, monks and nuns. We can never aspire to be more. A successful soldier or academic rises through the ranks. His life is shown to have value because he is promoted to being a professor or general. But that is not so with us. The only ladder in the Rule of St Benedict is that of humility. I am sure that monks, like friars, sometimes nurse secret desires for promotion, and dream of the glory of being cellarer or even abbot! I am sure that many a monk looks in the mirror and imagines what he might look like with a pectoral cross or even a mitre, and sketches a blessing when no-one is looking – he hopes! But we all know that the shape of our lives is really given not by promotion but by the journey to the Kingdom. The Rule is given, St Benedict says, to hasten us to our heavenly home.

I am reminded of a very beloved abbot who used to come and stay with our family every Christmas. He was admirable in every way, except for a slight tendency to take being an abbot rather too seriously, unlike anyone present today I am sure. He expected to be met at the railway station by the entire family, and for all six children to genuflect and kiss the abbatial ring, on Platform Four. This reverence was so ingrained in my family that a cousin of mine was reputed to often genuflect when she took her seat in the cinema! Every time our family abbot came to stay, there would be the annual fight about the celebration of Mass. He strongly maintained that as an abbot he had a right to four silver candlesticks, but my father always insisted that in his house every priest had the same number of candlesticks!

For most people in our society this makes no sense, for to live is to be in competition for success, to get ahead or perish. And so our lives are a puzzle, a question-mark. They apparently lead nowhere. One becomes a monk or a friar, and need be nothing more, ever. I remember that when I was elected Master of the Order, a well-known journalist wrote an article in the *NCR*, which concluded remarking that at the end of my term as Master, I would be only 55. 'What will Radcliffe do then?' he asked. When I read this I was disturbed. I felt as if the meaning of my life was being taken from me, and forced into other categories. What would Radcliffe do then? The implication was that my life should make sense through another 'promotion'. But why should I do anything except go on being a brother? Our lives have meaning because of an *absence* of progression, which points to God as the end and goal of our lives.

Once again, I wish to claim that it is in the singing of the Office that this claim makes sense. Earlier this year, I went into the cathedral church of Monereale in Sicily, beside the old Benedictine abbey. I had little free time but I had been told that whoever goes to Palermo and does not visit Monereale arrives a human and leaves a pig! And it was an astonishing experience. The whole interior is a dazzling jigsaw of mosaics which tell the history of creation and redemption. To enter the church is to find yourself inside the story, our story. This is humanity's true story, not the struggle to get to the top of the tree. This is a revelation of the structure of true time. The true story is not that of individual success, of promotion and competition; it is the story of humanity's journey to the Kingdom, celebrated every year in the liturgical cycle, from Advent to Pentecost, which climaxes in the green of ordinary time, our time.

This is *true* time, the time that encompasses all the little events and dramas of our lives. This is the time that gathers up all the little dramas of our lives, the small defeats and victories, and gives them sense. The monastic celebration of the liturgical year should be a disclosure of the true time, the only important story. The different times in the year – ordinary time, Advent, Christmas, Lent and Easter – should feel different, with different melodies, different colours, as different as the spring is from the summer, and summer from the autumn. They have to be distinctive enough to resist being dwarfed by the other rhythms: the financial year, the academic year; the years we count as we grow older. One of our brothers, Kim en Joong, the Korean Dominican painter, has made wonderful chasubles, which explode with the colours of the seasons.

Often the modern liturgy does not communicate this. When you go to Vespers, it could be any time of the year. But in our community in Oxford, where I lived for twenty years, we composed antiphons for every season of the year. I can still hear these when I travel. For me, Advent means certain hymn-tunes, antiphons for the *Benedictus* and the *Magnificat*. We know that Christmas is drawing near with the great O antiphons. Holy Week is the Lamentations of Jeremiah. We have to live the rhythm of the liturgical year as the deepest rhythm of our lives. The monastic liturgy is a reminder that where we are going is to the Kingdom. We do not know what will happen tomorrow or in the next century; we have no predictions to make, but our wisdom is to live for that ultimate end.

Perhaps I would add one final nuance. It is easy to say that the religious live for the coming of the Kingdom, but in actual fact often we do not. The liturgical year sketches the royal road to freedom, but we do not always take it. According to St Thomas, formation, especially moral formation, is always formation in freedom. But the entry into freedom is slow and painful, and will include mistakes, wrong choices, and sin. God brings us out of Egypt into freedom of the desert, but we become afraid and enslave ourselves to golden bulls, or try to sneak back to Egypt again. This is the true drama of the daily life of the monk, not whether he gets promoted up the ladder of office, but the initiation into freedom, with frequent collapses back into puerility and enslavement. How can we make sense of our slow ascension into God's freedom, and our frequent descents back into slavery? Once again, it is perhaps again in music that we may find the key.

St Augustine wrote that the history of humanity is like a musical score which gives a place for all the discords and disharmonies of human failure, but which finally leads to a harmonic resolution, in which everything has its place. In his wonderful work, *De Musica*, he wrote that 'Dissonance can be redeemed without being obliterated'.[6] The story of redemption is like a great symphony which embraces all our errors, our bum notes, and in which beauty finally triumphs. The victory is not that God wipes out our wrong notes, or pretends that they never happened, but that He finds a place for them in the musical score that redeems them. This happens above all in the Eucharist. In the words of Catherine Pickstock, 'the highest music in the fallen world, the redemptive music ... is none other than the repeated sacrifice of Christ himself which is the music of the forever-repeated Eucharist'.[7]

The Eucharist is the repetition of the climax in the drama of our liberation. Christ freely gives us his body, but the disciples reject him, deny him, run away from him, pretend that they do not know him. Here in the music of our relationship with God, we find the deepest disharmonies. But in the Eucharist they are taken up, embraced and transfigured into beauty in a gesture of love and gift. In this Eucharistic music we are made whole and find harmony. This is a harmonic resolution that does not wipe out our rejection of love and freedom, and pretends that they never happened, but transforms them into steps on the journey. In our celebrations we dare to remember those weak apostles.

So the meaning of the monk's life is that it goes to the Kingdom. Our story is the story of humanity on its way to the Kingdom. This we enact in the annual cycle of the liturgical year, from Creation to Kingdom. But the daily drama of the monk's life is more complex, with our struggles and failures to become free. The annual symphony of the journey to the Kingdom needs to be punctuated with the daily music of the Eucharist, which recognizes that we constantly refuse to walk to Jerusalem, to death and Resurrection, and choose instead unfreedom. Here we need to find ourselves every day in the music of the Eucharist, in which no disharmony is so crude as to be beyond God's creative resolution.

The space inside

Finally, we come to what is most fundamental in monastic life, what is most beautiful and hardest to describe, and that is humility. It is what is least immediately visible to the people who come to visit your monasteries, and yet it is the basis of everything. It is, Cardinal Hume says, 'a very beautiful thing to see, but the attempt to become

humble is painful indeed'.[8] It is humility that makes for God an
empty space in which God may dwell and his glory be seen. It is,
ultimately, humility which makes our communities the throne of
God.

It is hard for us today to find words to talk about humility. Our
society almost seems to invite us to cultivate the opposite; an
assertiveness, a brash self-confidence. The successful person
aggressively pushes himself forward. When we read in the seventh
step of humility that we must learn to say with the prophet 'I am a
worm and no man', then we flinch. But is this because we are so
proud? Or is it because we are so unsure of ourselves, so
unconfident of our value? Perhaps we dare not proclaim that we
are worms because we are haunted by the fear that we are worse
than worthless.

How are we to build communities which are living signs of
humility's beauty? How can we show the deep attractiveness of
humility in an aggressive world? You alone can answer that.
Benedict was the master of humility, and I am not sure that it has
always been the most obvious virtue of many Dominicans! But I
would like to share a brief thought. When we think of humility,
then it may be as an intensely personal and private thing: me looking
at myself and seeing how worthless I am, inspecting my own
inferiority, gazing at my own worm-like qualities. This is, to say the
least, a depressing prospect. Perhaps Benedict invites us to do
something far more liberating, which is to build a community in
which we are liberated from rivalry and competition and the
struggle for power. This is a new sort of community which is
structured by mutual deference, mutual obedience. This is a
community in which no-one is at the centre, but there is the empty
space, the void which is filled with the glory of God. This implies a
profound challenge to the modern image of the self which is of the
self as solitary, self-absorbed, the centre of the world, the hub
around which everything gravitates. At the heart of its identity is
self-consciousness: 'I think therefore I am'.

The monastic life invites us to let go of the centre, and to give in
to the gravitational pull of grace. It invites us to be de-centred.
Once again we find God disclosed in a void, an emptiness, and this
time at the centre of the community, the hollow space which is kept
for God. We have to make a home for the Word to come and dwell
among us, a space for God to be. As long as we are competing for

the centre, then there is no space for God. So then, humility is not me despising myself and thinking that I am awful; it is hollowing out the heart of the community, to make a space where the Word can pitch his tent.

What is the role of the abbot in this? I hesitate to say, since in the Dominican Order we have only ever had one abbot, a certain Matthew, and it was rather a disaster, so we have had no more. But perhaps all religious superiors have the role of ensuring that there is the space for God to be in the centre. Once again, I think that it is in the liturgy that we can find this beauty made manifest. God is enthroned on the praises of Israel. It is when people see monks singing the praise of God that they glimpse the freedom and the beauty of humility. In the Middle Ages, it was believed that good, harmonious music they went with building a harmonious community.[9] Music heals the soul and the community. We cannot sing together if each person is striving to sing more loudly, competing for the spotlight. In a similar way, I am sure that singing together in harmony, learning to sing one's own note, to find one's place in the melody, forms us as brethren, and shows to other people what it is like to live together without competition and rivalry. So the abbot will be the person who refuses to rush in and dominate the singing. He refuses to drown out the voices of the other monks, to grab the centre, to be the Pavarotti of the abbey. He will let the harmony rule. You can see how a community lives together when you hear it sing. And you can see immediately how different are Benedictines and Dominicans in their way of singing!

The climax of humility is when one discovers that not only is one not the centre of the world, but that one is not even the centre of oneself. There is not only a void in the centre of the community where God dwells, but there is a void at the centre of my being, where God can pitch his tent. I am a creature, to whom God gives existence at every moment. In the mosaics in Monereale, we see God making Adam. God gives Adam his breath and sustains him in being. At the heart of my being I am not alone. God is there breathing me into existence at every moment, giving me existence. At my centre there is no solitary self, no Cartesian ego but a space which is filled with God.

Perhaps this is the ultimate vocation of the monk, to show the beauty of that hollowness, to be, individually and communally, temples for God's glory to dwell in. You will not be surprised that I think that this is shown through the singing of the praises of God. And here I am really going beyond what I am competent to talk about, and will only have a go because it is fascinating. If you think I am talking nonsense, then you are probably right!

Every artistic creation echoes the first creation. In art we get our closest glimpse of what it means for God to have made the world from nothing. Its originality points back to that origin of all that is. Every poem, every painting, sculpture or song, gives us a hint of what it means for God to create. George Steiner wrote that

> Deep inside every art-act lies the dream of an absolute leap out of nothingness, of the invention of an enunciatory shape so new, so singular to its begetter, that it would, literally, leave the previous world behind.[10]

In the Christian tradition this has been especially true for music. St Augustine said that it is in music, in which sound comes forth from silence, that we can see what it means for the universe to be grounded in nothing, to be contingent, and so for us to be creatures. 'The alternation of sound and silence in music is seen by Augustine as a manifestation of the alternation of the coming into being and the passing into non-being which must characterise a universe created out of nothing'.[11] We hear in music, to quote Steiner again, 'the ever-renewed vestige of the original, never wholly accessible moment of creation ... the inaccessible first *fiat*'.[12] This is the echo of the big bang, or as Tavener said, the pre-echo of the divine silence.

At the heart of the monastic life is humility; not, I suspect, the grinding depressing humility of those who hate themselves; it is the humility of those who know that they are creatures, and that their existence is a gift. And so it is utterly right that at the centre of your life should be singing. For it is in this singing that we show forth God's bringing of everything to be. And you sing that Word of God, through which all is made. Here we can see a beauty which is more than just pleasing. It is the beauty which celebrates that we are made and remade. At the centre of our created selves God has made his home and his throne.

To conclude, I have argued in this conference that God's glory always needs a space, an emptiness, if it is to show itself: the emptiness between the wings of the cherubim in the temple; the empty tomb; a Jesus who vanishes in Emmaus. I have suggested that if you let such empty spaces be hollowed out in your lives, by being people who are not there for any particular reason, whose lives lead nowhere, and who face their creaturehood without fear, then your communities will be thrones for God's glory.

What we hope to glimpse in monasteries is more than we can say. The glory of God escapes our words. The mystery breaks our little ideologies. Like St Thomas Aquinas, we see that all that we can say is just straw. Does that mean that we can just be silent? No, because monasteries are not just places of silence but of song. We have to find ways of singing, at the limits of language, at the edge of meaning. This is what St Augustine calls the song of jubilation, and it is what we can learn to sing in the year of the Jubilee.

'You ask, what is singing in jubilation? It means to realize that words are not enough to express what we are singing in our hearts. At the harvest, in the vineyard, whenever men must labour hard, they begin with songs whose words express their joy. But when their joy brims over and words are not enough, they abandon even this coherence and give themselves up to the sheer sound of singing. What is this jubilation, this exultant song? It is the melody that means our hearts are bursting with feelings that words cannot express. And to whom does this jubilation most belong? Surely to God who is unutterable?'[13]

1   In Praise of Benedict, p. 23.
2   Aidan Nichols OP, *The Word Has Been Abroad* (Edinburgh, 1998, p. 1).
3   *To be a Pilgrim* (Slough, 1984, p. 39).
4   George Steiner, *Real Presences* (London, 1989, p. 145).
5   *De Musica VI*, xiv, 46.
6   Catherine Pickstock, 'Music: soul, and city and cosmos after Augustine'. *Radical Orthodoxy*, (ed. John Millbank, *et al.*) (London, 1999, p. 276, no. 131).
7   *Ibid.*, p. 265.
8   *To be a Pilgrim* (Slough, 1984, p. 67).
9   Cf: Pickstock, *op. cit.*, p. 262.
10 *Op. cit.*, p. 202.
11 Pickstock, *op. cit.*, p. 247.
12 Steiner, op cit, pp. 210, 202.
13 On Psalm 32, Sermon 1.8.

Consecrate them in Truth (John 17:17)[1]

Shortly after the foundation of the Order, almost 800 years ago, St Dominic scattered the brethren to the farthest ends of the known world, but he never imagined California. No-one can until they get here! He may been a friend of St Francis, but he never dreamed of San Francisco. And yet the arrival of the brothers and the sisters here 150 years ago was a sort of completion of that mission and a new beginning. Why was that?

We find the answer in the gospel chosen for today. Before he died, Jesus sends the disciples on their mission. As the Father sent him, so he sends them. This fragile and fearful little community is scattered. And yet they are to remain one as the Father and the Son are one, for they are to gather humanity into the unity of the Kingdom, God's own unity. The disciples are scattered and gathered together.

When Dominic dispersed the first sixteen brethren, to study and to preach, they resisted. They did not wish to break up their cosy little community in the south of France. But, for once, Dominic insisted. He had a vision of a new sort of religious order, perhaps the first of its kind, which would be sent to the ends of the world and yet remain one. The unity of the Order is part of our preaching of the one Kingdom. And that is why the Order has always remained one, unlike some others. It would make no sense to have a divided Order of Preachers.

When the brethren and the sisters of San Rafael arrived here on the West Coast, it was in a sense the end of the journey. Dominic could send us no further westward. But it was a new beginning, because here on the Pacific Rim all worlds meet. West meets east.

Here you can encounter every sort of culture, every nationality, every religious view, every crazy sect, every political option. How can we realize here Jesus' prayer that we shall all be one as he and the Father are one? This is the challenge here. How can we gather God's varied children into the unity of the Kingdom?

Today's gospel roots that unity in the truth. 'Consecrate them by means of the truth. Your word is truth.' The truth unites us. And *veritas*, truth, is the motto of the Order. It was this that brought me to the Order. When I left school, I became a friend for the first time of people who were not Christians, for the first time and who tried to convince me that my views were crazy. And the insistent question for me became: 'Is my faith true? If it is, then it must be the most important thing that there is. And if it is not, then I ought to be honest and give it all up.' At this point I remembered that there was an Order that had the motto 'Truth', and I decided that I wanted to join it. The problem was that I could not remember which Order it was. So I telephoned the Benedictines who had educated me and they told me it was the Dominicans. Within days I was in the Provincial's office, telling him that I wanted to join. Admittedly, it was a bit frustrating: he wanted to talk about football and I wanted to question him about transubstantiation. But here I am!

In the truth, we are one. But in the contemporary Church it is often claims to the truth that appear to divide rather than to unite us. Different groups within the Church claim special insight: conservatives, liberals, Thomists, feminists, liberation theologians. And we can be immensely intolerant of those who differ from us. There is a new stridency in the Church which threatens our witness to the Kingdom. I must say that I have not found the brethren and sisters here to be deeply split and divided. In fact you live together in remarkable peace. But if we are to be preachers of the Kingdom, we must still reflect on how to be bearers of the truth that overcomes divisions and unites.

I am always told that San Francisco is the land of tolerance. Anything is possible here. Tolerance is good, and we Christians could benefit from a lot more of it. But tolerance alone is not enough. Absolute tolerance fails to take the other person seriously. It is patronizing. I am told that 25 per cent of all Americans believe in reincarnation, but if someone tells me that they were Napoleon in a previous life, or that God is a green rabbit, then it is not enough to say: 'Well, if that is what makes you happy, then it is fine by me; just be comfortable with your feelings.' That is immensely condescending.

Jesus prays to the Father to consecrate the disciples in truth. God's truth consecrates, makes holy; it transforms us. We are tempted to make the truth something that we possess, our property. We wrap it up in a few formulas. We try to master it. And this is not surprising in a society which is dedicated to private property. Like everything else in the world, the truth has become something that you can possess.

But God's truth cannot be owned. It is a gift that cannot be mastered. It breaks open all our attempts to trap it in our words. It busts open our little ideologies. The word of God is truth that searches and probes us. It is a two-edged sword. De Chazal said that the Bible is not a book that we read; it reads us. It brings us face to face with the truth of who we are. It confronts us with the truth of the other person. It brings us to glimpse the inconceivable truth of the Holy God.

To be a preacher requires two apparently contradictory qualities: confidence and humility. We need the confidence of Paul who wrote in the second reading: 'If you confess with your heart that Jesus is Lord, and believe in your heart that God raised him from the dead, you will be saved.' There is a clear declaration. Without confidence, we cannot preach. We must dare boldly to proclaim our faith.

But also we need the humility of those who know that we know so little. As Thomas Aquinas said, of God we know nothing. We are mendicants for the truth, happy to beg a little bit of illumination from everyone whom we meet on the road. As Gregory of Nyssa said, we go from beginning to beginning to beginning. We must learn humility in the face of the other person's beliefs. They may be wrong in many ways, but they have something to teach us. Thomas remains a permanent inspiration for us Dominicans because he had a perfect balance of confidence and humility. He could write the *Summa Theologica* and claim that all that he had written was as straw. The mystery dissolves all arrogance.

I remember as an eager young student of theology in Oxford meeting a great Dominican theologian, Cornelius Ernst, on the staircase. It was the feast of the Assumption. And I stopped him and said, 'Come on Cornelius, please tell me in a few words what this feast is all about.' I was in a hurry and had no time to waste. It was time for breakfast. And he smiled and said, 'Oh dear. Go and buy a good bottle of wine and come and see me this evening.' By the end of the bottle I realized that was just the beginning.

Consecrate them in truth. This is a truth that heals and unites because it is a truth that transforms us, that undoes all our little claims to domination, explodes all ideologies, and breaks down the boundaries. It consecrates us in the love which is the life of God.

Many of the divisions between human beings, and even within the Church, spring from fear. We may absolutize our own positions because of a fear of those who are different. Fear hardens genuine insight into ideology. The traditionalist may fear that the tradition will be betrayed and the Church will fall into chaos, the feminist fears that the wisdom and value of women will be denied; the liberation theologian fears that the injustices of this world will be left unchallenged. These fears are perfectly understandable. I share them all.

But Jesus has prayed to the Father that we may be one in the truth, and Jesus' prayer is answered. He prays that the disciples may be protected by the most holy name, to which this Western Province of the brethren is dedicated. The Father hears him. We have no need to be afraid of anything. If we are indeed consecrated in the truth, then there is no need for anxiety. We have no need to take refuge in ideological fortresses from which to take pot shots at the other. We can dare to continue together on the pilgrimage towards the truth that makes us free and holy and one.

This was the confidence of Dominic, that courageous man. He sent the novices to preach; he took the risk of giving every brother a voice in the government of the Order. He sent us, brothers and sisters, to the ends of the earth, even as far as the West Coast of the United States. He trusted that the Lord will be with us. It is this trust that can make us preachers who are confident and humble, who know so much and so little.

Today we celebrate 150 years since the brethren and the sisters of San Rafael established the Order on the West Coast. I went to Benecia, to see the graveyard where nearly every sister and brother is buried. A few are buried elsewhere, such as Brother Joseph Alemany, the first Archbishop of San Francisco, who lies with his successors. There in the graveyard we are indeed one, in what one brother described as the perfectly united community. There are no ideological tiffs in the graveyard. Today we remember all those who have gone before us, all those previous generations, and celebrate our unity with them. This is not an ideological unity. They would have been surprised at much that we say and do, and a bit shocked that we do not get up at 3 a.m. to sing Matins, and that we eat meat. We would be equally surprised if we knew what those who will come after us will get up to! What unites us is a deeper truth that we can barely begin to imagine; a truth that consecrates us and draws us beyond all divisions; a truth which is the unutterable love which is God. This is the mystery we are called to preach.

1   Sermon for the 150th Anniversary of the Arrival of the Brethren and Sisters on the West Coast, 15 April 2000.

St Catherine of Siena (1347–80) Patroness of Europe

Note: A letter to the Dominican Order, published April 2000 to celebrate the naming of St Catherine of Siena as one of the Patrons of Europe.

During the Mass for the opening of the Second Synod for Europe, to my surprise and delight the Pope proclaimed St Catherine of Siena co-patroness of Europe, together with St Teresa Benedict of the Cross and St Bridget of Sweden. Catherine was a prodigious letter-writer to her brethren and sisters, and so it is appropriate to honour her in a brief letter to the Order.

Catherine's Europe was, like our world today, marked by violence and an uncertain future: the papacy had fled to Avignon, splitting the Church and dividing countries, cities and religious orders, including our own; cities were being decimated by the bubonic plague, known as the Black Death; there was a decline of vitality in the Church, a loss of a sense of purpose and a crisis of religious life.

Catherine refused to resign herself in the face of this suffering and division. In the words of Pope John Paul II, she dived 'into the thick of the ecclesiastical and social issues of her time'.[1] She addressed political and religious rulers, either in person or through letters, and clearly told them their faults and their Christian duty. She did not hesitate even to tell the Pope that he must be brave and go back to Rome. She went to the prisons and cared for the poor and the sick. She was consumed by an urgency to bring God's love and mercy to everyone.

Above all, Catherine struggled for peace. She was convinced that 'not by the sword or by war or by violence' could good be achieved, but 'through peace and through constant humble prayer'.[2] Yet she never sacrificed truth or justice for a cheap or easy peace. She reminded the rulers of Bologna that to seek peace without justice was like smearing ointment on a wound that needed to be cauterized.[3] She knew that to be a peacemaker was to follow the steps of Christ, who made peace between God and humanity. And thus the peacemaker must sometimes face Christ's own fate, and suffer rejection. The peacemaker is 'another Christ crucified'. Our own world is also torn by violence: ethnic and tribal violence in Africa and the Balkans; the threat of nuclear war; violence in our cities and families. Catherine invites us to have the courage to be peacemakers, even if this means that we must suffer persecution and rejection ourselves.

Peace, for Catherine, meant, above all, peace in the Church, the healing of the Great Schism. Here we see both her intense love of the Church, which for her was 'no other than Christ himself',[4] and her courage and freedom. She so loved the Church that she did not hesitate to denounce the failings of the clergy and bishops in their pursuit of wealth and position, and called for the Church to be the mystery of Christ in the world, the humble servant of all. She even dared to tell God what to do, when she prayed:

> You know how and you are able and it is your will,
> so I plead with you to have mercy on the world,
> and to restore the warmth of charity and peace
> and unity to holy Church. It is my will that you
> do not delay any longer.[5]

The Church in our time also suffers from divisions, caused by misunderstanding, intolerance and a loss of 'the warmth of charity and peace'. Today the love of the Church is often assumed to mean an uncritical silence. One must not 'rock the boat'! But Catherine could never be silent. She wrote to some cardinals, 'Be silent no longer. Cry out with a hundred thousands voices. I see that the world is destroyed through silence. Christ's spouse is pallid, her colour has been drained from her.'[6] May St Catherine teach us her deep love of the Body of Christ, and the wisdom and courage to speak truthfully and openly with words that unite rather than divide, which illuminate rather than obscure, and which heal rather than wound.

Catherine's relationships with her friends, and especially her Dominican brothers and sisters, was marked by the same combination of love and boldness of speech ('parrhesia', e.g. Acts 4:31, 2 Cor 7:4). She regarded each friend as a gift from God, to be loved 'very closely, with a particular love'.[7] She believed that their mutual friendship was an opportunity 'to bring each other to birth in the gentle presence of God',[8] and a proclamation of 'the glory and praise of God's name to others'. But this love did not prevent her from speaking very frankly to her friends, and telling her brethren exactly what they should do, including her beloved Raymond of Capua, who became Master of the Order in the year of her death. There can be no love without truth, nor truth without love. This is how she prayed for her friends:

> Eternal God,
> I pray to you
> for all those you have given me
> to love with a special love
> and with special concern.
> Let them be illuminated with your light.
> Let all imperfection be taken from them,
> so that in truth
> they may work in your garden,
> where you have assigned them.[9]

If the Dominican Family is to become, in Catherine's words, 'a very spacious, gladsome and fragrant, a most delightful garden',[10] then we must learn both her capacity for mutual friendship and for truthfulness. Our friendship as men and women, religious and lay people, is a great gift for the Order and for the Church, but it often is marred by wounds of which we hardly dare to speak. If we are to work together as preachers of the gospel, then we must speak to each other with Catherine's frankness and trust, so that 'in truth they may work in your garden'.

Catherine was a passionate woman with big desires: for union with God, for the spread of the gospel and for the good of the whole human family. Desire expands our hearts. She told God: 'you make the heart big, not stingy – so big that it has room in its loving charity for everyone'.[11] God said to Catherine, 'I who am infinite God want you to serve me with what is infinite, and you have nothing infinite except your soul's desire.'[12]

How can we grow as men and women who are touched by Catherine's passion for God? How can we be liberated from smallness of heart and contentment with little satisfactions? Perhaps it is through discovering, as did Catherine, that God is present in the very centre of our being and identity. The passion for God is not a taste to be acquired, like a love of football. It is there in the core of my being, waiting to be discovered. Our world is marked by a deep hunger for identity. For many people today the urgent question is: 'Who am I?' This was Catherine's question. The contemporary search for self-knowledge is often a narcissistic preoccupation with self, an introverted concentration on one's own well-being and fulfilment. But for Catherine, when I finally see myself as I am, I do not discover a little nugget of lonely selfhood. In what Catherine called 'the cell of self-knowledge' I discover myself being loved into existence. She described herself as 'dwelling in the cell of self-knowledge in order to know better God's goodness towards her'.[13] If I dare to make that journey towards self-knowledge, then I shall discover how small, flawed and finite I am, but I shall also see that I am utterly loved and valued. God told Catherine: 'It was with providence that I created you, and when I contemplated my creature in myself, I fell in love with the beauty of my creation.'[14]

So Catherine offers a liberating answer to the contemporary quest for identity. It takes us far away from a false identity based on status or wealth or power. For at the heart of our being is the God whose love sustains us in being. This is the place of contemplative prayer, where one meets the God who delights in loving and forgiving, and whose own goodness we taste. Here we discover the secret of Catherine's peace and her dynamism, her confidence and her humility. This is what made this young woman, with little formal education, a great preacher. This is what gave her the freedom to speak and to listen. This is what gave her the courage to dive in and address the great issues of her time. With the help of her prayers we may do likewise.

1   Apostolic Letter, *L'Osservatore Romano*, no. 40 (1611), English edition.
2   D. 15.
3   L. 268.
4   L. 171.
5   O. 24.
6   L. 16.

7 D. 41.
8 L. 292.
9 O. 21.
10 D. 158.
11 O. 21.
12 D. 92.
13 D. 1.
14 D. 135.

Part Three

Mission

Mission to a Runaway World: Future Citizens of the Kingdom

Note: This was the keynote address given in December 2000 to SEDOS, the international organization of all missionary institutions of the Catholic Church.

I have been asked to reflect upon a spirituality of mission for our globalized world. What does it mean to be a missionary in Disneyland? When I was asked to give this lecture I was delighted, because it is a fascinating topic, but I was also hesitant, because I have never been a missionary in the usual sense of the word. At the elective General Chapter of the Order in Mexico, eight years ago, the brethren identified the criteria for candidates to be Master of the Order. Crucially, he should have pastoral experience outside his own country. They then elected me who had only ever been an academic in England. I do not know whether all congregations act so eccentrically, but it shows why I feel rather unfitted to give this lecture.

What is so new about our world, that we must look for a new spirituality of mission? How is it so different from the world to which previous generations of missionaries were sent? We may reply, automatically, that what is new is globalization. E-mails stream into our offices from all over the world. Trillions of dollars circulate around the markets of the world every day. As it is so often said, we live in a global village. Missionaries are no longer dispatched on ships to unknown countries; almost everywhere is no more than a day's journey away. But I wonder if 'globalization' really identifies the new context for mission. The global village is the fruit of an historical evolution that has been taking place for at least 500, if not 5000, years. Some experts argue that in many ways the world 100 years ago was just as globalized as today.

Perhaps what is really distinctive about our world is a particular fruit of globalization, which is that we do not know where the world is going. We do not have a shared sense of the direction of our history. Tony Blair's guru, Anthony Giddens, calls it 'the runaway world.'[1] History appears to be out of our control, and we do not know where we are heading. It is for this runaway world that we must discover a vision and a spirituality of mission.

The first great missions of the Church outside Europe were linked with the colonialism of the sixteenth to the twentieth centuries.[2] The Spanish and the Portuguese brought their mendicant friars with them; just the Dutch and the English took their Protestant missionaries. The missionaries may have supported or criticized the Conquistadors, but there was a shared sense of where history was going, towards the western domination of the world. That gave the context of mission. In the second half of the twentieth century, mission occurred within a new context, that of conflict between the two great power-blocs of east and west, of communism and capitalism. Some missionaries may have prayed for the triumph of the proletariat, and others for the defeat of godless communism, but this conflict was the context of mission.

Now, with the fall of the Berlin Wall, we do not know where we are going. Are we going towards universal wealth, or is the economic system about to collapse? Will we have the Long Boom or the Big Bang? Will the Americans dominate the world economy for centuries, or are we at the end of a brief history when the west was at the centre of the world? Will the global community expand to include everyone, including the forgotten continent of Africa, or will the global village shrink, and leave most people outside? Is it global village or global pillage? We do not know.

We do not know, because globalization has reached a new stage, with the introduction of technologies whose consequences we cannot guess. We do not know because, according to Giddens,[3] we have invented a new sort of risk. Human beings have always had to cope with risk: the risk of plagues, bad harvests, storms, drought and the occasional invasions of barbarians. But these were largely external risks that were out of our control. You never knew when a meteorite might hit the planet, or a flee-ridden rat might not arrive with the bubonic plague. But now we are principally at risk from what we ourselves have done, what he calls 'manufactured risk': global warming, overpopulation, pollution, unstable markets, the unforeseen consequences of genetic engineering. We do not know the effects of what we are now doing. We live in a runaway world. This produces profound anxiety. We Christians have no special knowledge about the future. We do not know any more than anyone else whether we are on the way to war or peace, prosperity or poverty. We, too, are often haunted by the anxiety of our contemporaries. I happen to be deeply optimistic about the future of humanity, but is this because I have inherited St Thomas's belief in the deep goodness of humanity, or my mother's optimistic genes?

In this runaway world, what Christians offer is not knowledge but wisdom, the wisdom of humanity's ultimate destination, the Kingdom of God. We may have no idea of how the Kingdom will come, but we believe in its triumph. The globalized world is rich in knowledge. Indeed, one of the challenges of living in this cyberworld is that we are drowned with information, but there is little wisdom. There is little sense of humanity's ultimate destiny. Indeed, such is our anxiety about the future that it is easier not to think about it all. Let us grab the present moment. Let us eat, drink and be merry for tomorrow we may die. So our missionary spirituality must be sapiential, the wisdom of the end to which we are called, a wisdom which liberates us from anxiety.

In this lecture I wish to suggest that the missionary may be the bearer of this wisdom in three ways, through presence, epiphany and through proclamation. In some places all we can do is to be present, but there is a natural thrust towards making our hope visible and our wisdom explicit. The Word has become flesh and now in our mission the flesh becomes word.[4]

Presence

A missionary is sent. That is the meaning of the word. But to whom are missionaries sent in our runaway world? When I was a schoolboy with the Benedictines, missionaries came to visit us from faraway places, like Africa and the Amazon. We saved up our money so that children would be baptized with our names. There should be hundreds of middle-aged Timothys around the world. So

missionaries were sent from the west to other places. But from
where are missionaries sent these days? They used to come especially
from Ireland, Spain, Brittany, Belgium and Quebec. But few
missionaries are from those countries today. The modern missionary
is more likely to come from India or Indonesia. I remember the
excitement in the British press when the first missionary arrived in
Scotland from Jamaica. So in our globalized village there is no
centre from which missionaries are despatched. In the geography of
the World Wide Web there is no centre, at least in theory. In fact,
we know that there are more telephone lines in Manhattan than in
sub-Saharan Africa.

As the beginning of an answer, I would suggest that in this new
world missionaries are sent to those who are other than us, who are
distant from us because of their culture, faith or history. They are far
away, but not necessarily physically distant. They are strangers
though they may be our neighbours. The expression 'the global
village' sounds cosy and intimate, as if we all belong to one big
happy human family. But our global world is traversed by splits and
fractures which make us foreign to each other, incomprehensible
and even, sometimes, enemies. The missionary is sent to be in these
places. Pierre Claverie, the Dominican bishop of Oran in Algeria,
was assassinated by a bomb in 1996. Just before he died he wrote.

> L'Eglise accomplit sa vocation quand elle est présente aux ruptures qui
> crucifient l'humanité dans sa chair et son unité. Jésus est mort écartelé
> entre ciel et terre, bras étendus pour rassembler les enfants de Dieu
> dispersés par le péché qui les sépare, les isole et les dresse les uns contre
> les autres et contre Dieu lui-même. Il s'est mis sur les lignes de fracture
> nées de ce péché. En Algérie, nous sommes sur l'une de ces lignes
> sismiques qui traversent le monde: Islam/Occident, Nord/Sud, riches/
> pauvres. Nous y sommes bien à notre place car c'est en ce lieu là que
> peut s'entrevoir la lumière de la Résurrection.[5]

These lines of fracture do not run just between parts of the world:
the north and the south, the developed world and the so-called
developing world. These lines traverse every country and every city:
New York and Rome, Nairobi and Sao Paolo, Delhi and Tokyo.
They divide those who have clean water and those who do not,
those who have access to the Internet and those who do not, the
literate and the illiterate; the left and the right, those of different
faiths and none, black and white. The missionary is to be the bearer

of a wisdom, of God's 'purpose which he set forth in Christ as a plan for the fullness of time, to unite all things in him, things in heaven and things on earth' (Ephesians 1:10). And this wisdom we represent by being present to those who are divided from us by the walls of division.

But we must take a further step. Being a missionary is not what I do; it is who I am. Just as Jesus is the one who is sent (Hebrews 3:1). Being present to the other – living on the lines of fracture – implies a transformation of who I am. In being with and for that other person I discover a new identity. I think of an old Spanish missionary whom I met in Taiwan, who had worked in China for many years and who had suffered imprisonment. Now he was old and sick, and his family wished him to return to Spain. But he said, 'I cannot go back. I *am* Chinese. I would be a stranger in Spain.' When John XXIII met a group of American Jewish leaders in 1960, he astonished them by walking into the room and saying, 'I am Joseph, your brother.' This is who I am, and I cannot be myself without you. So, being sent implies a dying to who one was. One lets go of a little identity. Chrys McVey, one of my American brethren, who lives in Pakistan, was asked how long he would remain there, and he replied, 'Until I am tired of dying.' To be present for, and with, the other is a sort of dying, so as to be a sign of the Kingdom in which we will be one.

Nicholas Boyle wrote that 'the only morally defensibly and conceptually consistent answer to the question "Who are we now?" is "Future citizens of the world" '.[6] We are not just people who work for a new world order, who try to overcome war and division. Who we are *now* is future citizens of the world. One could adapt Boyle's words and say that *now* we are the future citizens of the Kingdom. The Kingdom is my country. Now I discover who I am to be by being close to those who are farthest away. It is precisely our Catholicism which pushes us beyond every small and sectarian identity, every narrow little sense of myself, to that which we can barely glimpse now. That is the embodiment of our wisdom.

This is not easy, and, above all, it requires fidelity. The missionary is not a tourist. The tourist can go to exotic places, take photographs, enjoy the food and the views, and go back home proudly bearing T-shirts. The missionary is only a sign of the Kingdom in staying there. As one of my brethren said, 'You do not only unpack your bags, you throw your bags away.'

I do not mean that every missionary must stay until death. There may be many good reasons to leave: a new challenge to be faced elsewhere, illness or exhaustion, and so on. But I am suggesting that mission implies some conception of fidelity. It is the fidelity of a Spanish missionary whom I met in the Peruvian Amazon, who just goes on being there year after year, visiting his people, making his way around the little settlements, faithfully remaining, even if not much appears to happen. Often the pain of the missionary is discovering that one is not wanted. Maybe the local people, or even the local vocations to one's order, wait for him or her to go. It is the stamina to go on being there, sometimes unappreciated. The heroism of the missionary is in daring to discover who I am with and for these others, even if they do not wish to discover who they are with and for me. It is remaining there faithfully, even if it may cost one one's life, as it did for Pierre Claverie and the Trappist monks in Algeria.

I escaped from Rome just before the World Youth Day. But in my meeting there with some of the young Dominican laity I was struck by their delight in being with those who are different, who are unlike themselves. Germans and French, Poles and Pakistanis, there is an astonishing openness which reaches across the boundaries of race and culture and generation and faith. This is a gift of the young to the mission of the Church, and a sign of the Kingdom. Perhaps the challenge for the young missionary is learning that stamina, that enduring fidelity to the other, faced with our own fragility and anxiety. Our houses of formation should be schools of fidelity, where we learn to hang in there, stay put, even when we fail, even when there are misunderstandings, crises in relationship, even when we feel that our brethren or sisters are not faithful to us. The answer is not then to run away, to start again, to join another Order or to get married. We have to unpack our bags and throw them away. Presence is not merely being there. It is staying there. It takes the form of a life lived through history, the shape of a life that points to the Kingdom. The enduring presence of the missionary is indeed a sign of the Real Presence of the Lord who gave his body to us forever.

Epiphany

In many parts of the world, all that the missionary can do is to be there. In some Communist and Islamic countries nothing more is possible, just being an implicit sign of the Kingdom. Sometimes in our inner cities, or working with the young or the alienated, the mission must begin anonymously. The worker-priest is simply there in the factory. But our faith yearns to take visible form, to be seen. This year Neil MacGregor, the Director of the National Gallery in London, organized an exhibition called 'Seeing Salvation'. For most of European history our faith has been made visible, in glass, painting and sculpture. The celebration of Christ's birth used to begin with Epiphany, the disclosure of the glory of God among us. When Simeon receives the child Jesus in the Temple he rejoices, 'for my eyes have seen thy salvation which you have prepared in the presence of all peoples' (Luke 2:31 f.). As St John says, we proclaim 'that which we have heard, and which we have seen with our eyes, which we have looked upon and touched with our hands' (1 John 1:1f.). Mission pushes beyond presence to Epiphany.

Ever since the Iconoclastic Controversy in the ninth century, Christianity has sought to show God's face. In Europe in the Middle Ages, people rarely saw the image of any face except those of Christ and the saints, but in our world we are bombarded by faces. We have new icons on our walls: Madonna, Princess Diana, Tiger Woods, the Spice Girls. To be someone important today is to achieve 'icon status'! Everywhere there are faces: politicians, actors, footballers, the rich, people who are famous just for being famous. They smile at us from the billboards in our streets and on our television screens. But we believe that all of humanity hungers to see another face, the face of God, the beatific vision. How can we manifest that face?

It would not be enough just to add Christ's face to the crowd. It would be good but insufficient for Walt Disney to make a cartoon of the gospels. Putting Jesus' face on the screen with Mickey Mouse and Donald Duck would not achieve Epiphany. Many Protestant churches in Britain have signs outside their churches with the words of the gospel competing with the adverts in the streets. This may be admirable, but I always find it rather embarrassing. I remember our giggles as children when we drove past the sign outside a local church which asked whether we watched with the wise virgins or slept with the foolish virgins.

The challenge is this: How can we disclose the glory of God, God's beauty? In this world filled with images, how can God's beauty be manifested? Balthasar talks of the 'self-evidence' of beauty, 'its intrinsic authority'.[7] We recognise in beauty a summons that we cannot easily ignore. This beauty has the authority of the author of heaven and earth. C. S. Lewis said that beauty rouses up the desire for 'our own far-off country',[8] the home for which we long and have never seen. Beauty discloses our ultimate end, that for which we are made, our wisdom. In this runaway world, with its unknown future, the missionary is the bearer of wisdom, the wisdom of humanity's final destiny. This final destiny is glimpsed in the beauty of God's face. How can we show it now?

This question is easier to ask than to answer; I hope that you may be able to come up with some more stimulating answers than I have! I would suggest that we need to present images, faces which are different in type from the faces that we see in our streets. In the first place, beauty is disclosed not in the faces of the rich and the famous but the poor and the powerless. And secondly, the images of the global village offer entertainment, distraction, whereas the beauty of God is disclosed in transformation.

The images of the global village show the beauty of power and wealth. It is the beauty of the young and the fit who have everything. It is the beauty of a consumerist society. Now, do not think that I am jealous of the young and fit, however nostalgic I may be, but the gospels locate beauty elsewhere. The disclosure of the glory of God is the cross, a dying and deserted man. This is such a scandalous idea that it seems to have taken 400 years for this to be represented. Possibly the first representation of the crucified Christ is on the doors of Santa Sabina where I live, which were made in 432 after the destruction of Rome by the barbarians. God's irresistible beauty shines through utter poverty.

This may seem a crazy idea, until one thinks of one of the most attractive and beautiful of all saints, St Francis of Assisi. I made a little pilgrimage to Assisi this summer. The Basilica was filled with crowds who were drawn by the beauty of his life. The frescoes of Giotto are lovely, but the deeper loveliness is that of *il poverello*. His life is hollowed by a void, a poverty, which can only be filled by God. Cardinal Suhard wrote that to be a missionary 'does not consist in engaging in propaganda nor even in stirring people up, but in being a living mystery. It means to live in such a way that one's life would make no sense if God did not exist'.[9] We see God's beauty in Francis, because his life would make no sense if God did not exist.

Just as important, Francis found an new image for God's own poverty (though why I am doing all this advertising for the Franciscans, I cannot imagine!). Neil MacGregor says that it was Francis who invented the crib, the sign of God embracing our poverty. In 1223 he wrote to the Lord of Greccio,

> I would like to represent the birth of the Child just as it took place at Bethlehem, so that people should see with their own eyes the hardships He suffered as an infant, how He was laid on hay in a manger with the ox and the ass standing by.[10]

In the world of the thirteenth-century Renaissance, with its new frescoes, new exotic consumer goods, its new urban civilization, its mini-globalization, Francis revealed the beauty of God with a new image of poverty.

That is our challenge in the global village, to show the beauty of the poor and powerless God. It is especially hard because often our mission is in the places of most terrible poverty; in Africa, Latin America and parts of Asia, where poverty is evidently ugly. Missionaries build schools, universities and hospitals. We run powerful and absolutely vital institutions. We are seen as rich. But in many countries the health and educational system would collapse if it were not for the Church. How then can we show the beauty of the glory of God, visible in poverty? How can we offer these irreplaceable services and still lead lives which are mysteries and which make no sense without God?

I now glance quickly at a second way in which we can manifest God's beauty, and that is through acts of transformation. I begun this lecture by suggesting that what is perhaps unique about our world is not so much that it is global, as that we do not know where it is going. We have no idea what sort of future we are creating for ourselves. Even the North Pole has melted and become a pool of water. What next? This uncertainty provokes a deep anxiety. We hardly dare to even contemplate the future, and so it is easier to live just for now. This is the culture of instant gratification. As Kessler writes,

> Most people live today less from great overarching hopes and perspectives than from short-term intentions and tangible goals.

> Experience your life – now is the imperative of the secondary culture
> which now spans the globe. It is enough to live life like this, in the
> present – without a goal.[11]

When I fly into London, I often see the Millennium Wheel, the city's proud celebration of 2000 years since the birth of Christ. But all it does is to go round and round. It goes nowhere. It offers us the chance to be spectators, who observe the world without commitment. It entertains us, and enables us to momentarily escape the hectic city. It is a good symbol of how often we seek to survive in this runaway world. We are content to be entertained, to escape a while. And this is what so many of our images offer, entertainment which lets us forget.[12] Computer games, soap operas and films offer us amnesia in the face of an unknown future. Mind you, I am still waiting for one of my nieces to take me on the Millennium Wheel!

This escapism is above all expressed in that late twentieth-century phenomenon, the 'happening'. There is even the French word for it, '*Le* happening'. When France celebrated the millennium with a 1000-kilometre breakfast, it was '*un incroyable* happening'! A happening may be a disco, a football match, a concert, a party, a fiesta, the Olympics. A happening is a moment of exuberance, of ecstasy, where we are transported out of our dull, unmalleable world, so that we can forget. When Disneyland built a new town in Florida, in which people could try to escape from the anxieties of modern America, it was named Celebration.

But Christianity finds its centre also in '*un incroyable* happening', which is the Resurrection. But it is an utterly different sort of happening. It does not offer escapism, but transformation. It does not invite us to forget tomorrow, but is the future breaking in now. Faced with all our anxiety in this runaway world, not knowing where we are going, Christians cannot respond either with amnesia or with optimistic predications about the future. But we find signs of the Resurrection breaking in with gestures of transformation and liberation. Our celebrations are not an escape but a foretaste of the future. They offer not opium, as Marx thought, but promise.

An English Dominican, called Cornelius Ernst, once wrote that the experience of God is what he calls the 'genetic moment'. The genetic moment is transformation, newness, creativity, in which God errupts into our lives. He wrote.

> Every genetic moment is a mystery. It is dawn, discovery, spring, new

birth, coming to the light, awakening, transcendence, liberation, ecstasy, bridal consent, gift, forgiveness, reconciliation, revolution, faith, hope, love. It could be said that Christianity is the consecration of the genetic moment, the living centre from which it reviews the indefinitely various and shifting perspectives of human experience in history. That, at least, is or ought to be its claim: that it is the power to transform and renew all things: 'Behold, I make all things new'. (Apoc. 21:5)[13]

So the challenge for our mission is how to make God visible through gestures of freedom, liberation, transformation, little 'happenings' that are signs of the end. We need little erruptions of God's uncontainable freedom and his victory over death. Strangely enough, I have found it easier to think of rather obvious secular images than religious ones: the small figure in front of the tank in Tienanmen Square, the fall of the Berlin Wall.

What might be explicitly religious images? Perhaps a community of Dominican nuns in northern Burundi, Tutsis and Hutus living and praying together in peace in a land of death. The little monastery, surrounded by the greenery of cultivated fields in a countryside that is burnt and barren, is a sign of God, who does not let death have the last word. Another example might be an ecumenical community which I visited in Belfast, Northern Ireland. Catholics and Protestants lived together, and when anyone was killed in the sectarian battles, then a Catholic and a Protestant would go from the community to visit the relatives, and to pray with them. This community was an embodiment of our wisdom, a sign that we are not fated to violence, a little epiphany of the Kingdom. We do not know whether peace is around the corner or whether the violence will get worse, but here was a word made flesh which spoke of God's ultimate purpose.

Proclamation

We have progressed from mission as presence to mission as epiphany. Our eyes have seen the salvation of the Lord. But we must make one last step, which is to proclamation. Our gospel must come to word. At the end of Matthew's Gospel, the disciples are sent out to all the nations to make disciples, and to teach all that Jesus has commanded. The Word becomes flesh, but the flesh also becomes Word.

Here we encounter what is perhaps the deepest crisis in our

mission today. There is a profound suspicion of anyone who claims to teach, unless they come from the East or have some strange New Age doctrine. Missionaries who teach are suspected of indoctrination, of cultural imperialism, of arrogance. Who are we to tell anyone what they should believe? To teach that Jesus is God is seen as indoctrination, whereas to teach that God is a sacred mushroom is part of the rich tapestry of human tradition! Anyway, our society is deeply sceptical of any truth claims. We live in Disneyland, in which the truth can be reinvented as we wish. In the virtual age, the truth is what you conjure up on your computer screen. I read of a pilot who took off from an airport in Peru, but all his controls went crazy. When he turned left, the controls said that he was going right; when he went up, they said that he was going down. His last recorded words were 'It's all fiction.' Alas, the mountain he hit was not.

In *Christianity Rediscovered*, Vincent Donovan describes how he worked for many years as a missionary with the Maasai, building schools and hospitals, but never proclaiming his faith. He was not encouraged to do so by his superiors. Finally, he could restrain himself no longer and he gathered together the people and told them about his belief in Jesus. And then (if I remember correctly, since my copy of the book is lost) the elders said, 'We always wondered why you were here, and now at last we know. Why did you not tell us before?' This is why we are sent, to bring our faith to word, to proclaim the truth. We do not always have the freedom to speak, and we must choose well the moment, but it would ultimately be patronizing and condescending not to proclaim what we believe to be true. Indeed, it is part of the good news that human beings are made for the truth and can attain it. As *Fides et Ratio* puts it, 'One may define the human being ... as the one who seeks the truth' (para. 28), and that search is not in vain. We have, as the Dominican Constitutions say, a *propensio ad veritatem*, (LCO 77.2), an inclination to the truth. Any spirituality of mission has to include a passion for the truth.

At the same time, it is central to traditional Catholic teaching that we stand at the very limits of language, barely glimpsing the edge of the mystery. St Thomas says that the object of faith is not the words we speak, but God whom we cannot see and know. The object of our faith is beyond the grasp and dominion of our words. We do not own the truth or master it. Faced with the beliefs and claims of others we must have a profound humility. As Claverie wrote, *Je ne possède pas la vérité, j'ai besoin de la vérité des autres* ('I am a beggar after the truth').

At the heart of a spirituality of mission is surely an understanding of the right relationship between the *confidence* that we have in the revelation of the truth and the *humility* that we have before the mystery. The missionary must seek that right integration between confidence and humility. This is a source of an immense tension within the Church, between the Congregation for the Doctrine of the Faith and some Asian theologians, and indeed within many religious orders. It can be a fruitful tension at the heart of our proclamation of the mystery. I remember a General Chapter of the Dominicans in which a fierce argument broke out between those who staked their whole lives and vocations on the proclamation of the truth, and those who stressed how little Aquinas thought we could know of God. It ended with a seminar in the bar on a text of the *Summa contra Gentiles*, and the consumption of much beer and cognac! To live that tension well, between proclamation and dialogue, I believe that the missionary needs a spirituality of truthfulness and a life of contemplation.

It may appear strange to talk of a spirituality of truthfulness. Obviously, the preacher must say only what is true. But I believe that one will only know when to speak and when to be silent – that balance of confidence and humility – if one has been trained in acute discipline of truthfulness. This is a slow and painful asceticism, becoming attentive to one's use of words, in one's attention to what others say, in an awareness of all the ways in which we use words to dominate, to subvert, to manipulate rather than to reveal and disclose.

Nicholas Lash wrote:

> Commissioned as ministers of God's redemptive Word, we are required, in politics and in private life, in work and in play, in commerce and scholarship, to practise and foster that philology, that word-caring, that meticulous and conscientious concern for the quality of conversation and the truthfulness of memory, which is the first causality of sin. The Church accordingly is, or should be, a school of philology, an academy of word-care.[14]

The idea of the theologian as a philologist sounds very dry and dusty. How can a missionary have time for that sort of a thing? But to be a preacher is to learn the asceticism of truthfulness in all the words we speak, how we talk about other people, our friends and our enemies, people when they have left the room, the Vatican, ourselves. It is only if we learn this truth in the heart that we will be able to tell the difference between a good confidence in the proclamation of the truth, and the arrogance of those who claim to know more than they can; between humility in the face of the mystery and a wishy-washy relativism which does not dare to speak at all. The discipline is part of our assimilation to the one who is the Truth, and whose word 'is living and active, sharper than any two-edged sword, piercing to the division of soul and spirit, of joints and marrow, and discerning the thoughts and intentions of the heart' (Hebrews 4: 12).

Secondly, we will only be confident and humble preachers if we become contemplative. Chrys McVey said that 'Mission begins in humility and ends in mystery.' It is only if we learn to rest in God's silence, that we can discover the right words; words that are neither arrogant nor vacuous; words that are both truthful and humble. It is only if the centre of our lives is God's own silence that we will know when language ends and when silence begins; when to proclaim and when to be quiet. Rowan Williams wrote that

> What we must rediscover is the discipline of silence – not an absolute, unbroken inarticulacy, but the discipline of letting go of our own easy chattering about the gospel so that our words may come again from a new and different depth or force from something beyond our fantasies.[15]

It is this contemplative dimension that destroys the false images of God that we may be tempted to worship, and which liberates us from the traps of ideology and arrogance.

Future Citizens of the Kingdom

I must now conclude by gathering together the threads. I have suggested that the beginning of all mission is presence; it is being there as a sign of the Kingdom, with those who are most different, separated from us by history, culture or faith. But this is just the beginning. Our mission pushes us towards epiphany and ultimately to proclamation. The Word becomes flesh, and flesh becomes word. Each stage in the development of our mission asks of the missionary different qualities: fidelity, poverty, freedom, truthfulness and silence. Am I offering a picture of an impossibly saintly missionary, unlike any actual missionary? Does this add up to a coherent 'spirituality of mission'?

I have suggested that at this stage in the history of the Church's mission, we might best think of the missionary as the future citizen of the Kingdom. Our runaway world is out of control. We do not know where it is going, whether to happiness or misery, to prosperity or poverty. We Christians have no privileged information. But we do believe that ultimately the Kingdom will come. That is our wisdom, and it is a wisdom that missionaries embody in their very lives.

St Paul writes to the Philippians that, 'forgetting what lies behind and straining forward to what lies ahead, I press on toward the goal for the prize of the upward call of God in Christ Jesus' (Phil 3:13f.). This is a wonderfully dynamic image. St Paul is stretched out, pressed forward like an Olympic athlete in Sydney going for gold! To be a future citizen of the Kingdom is to live by this dynamism. It is to be stretched, reaching out, pressed forward. The missionary endures incompletion; he or she is half made until the Kingdom, when all will be one. We stretch out to the other, to those most distant, incomplete until we are one with them in the Kingdom. We reach out for a fullness of truth, which now we only glimpse dimly; all that we proclaim is haunted by silence. We are hollowed out by a longing for God, whose beauty may be glimpsed in our poverty. To be a future citizen of the Kingdom is to be dynamically, radiantly, joyfully incomplete.

Eckhart wrote that, 'just as much as you go out of all things, just so much, neither more nor less, does God come enter in with all that is His – if indeed you go right out of all that is yours'.[16] The beauty of Eckhart is that the less one knows what he is talking about, the more wonderful it sounds! Perhaps he is inviting us to that radical exodus from ourselves, that makes a hollow for God to enter. We stretch out to God in our neighbour, God who is most other, so to discover God in the centre of our being, God as most inward. For God is utterly other and utterly inward, which is why, to love God, we must both love our neighbour and ourselves.

This love is very risky. Giddens says that in this dangerous world, careering away towards an unknown future, the only solution is to take risks. Risk is the characteristic of a society that looks to the future. He says that 'a positive embrace of risk is the very source of that energy which creates wealth in a modern economy ... Risk is the mobilising dynamic of a society bent on change, that wants to determine its own future rather than leaving it to religion, tradition, or the vagaries of nature.'[17] He clearly sees religion as a refuge from risk, but our mission invites us to a risk beyond his imagining. This is the risk of love. It is the risk of living for the other who might not want me; the risk of living for a fullness of truth, that I cannot capture; the risk of letting myself be hollowed out by yearning for the God whose Kingdom will come. This is most risky and yet most sure.

1   *Runaway World: How Globalisation is reshaping our lives* (London, 1999).
2   On the first two stages of mission, cf. Robert J. Schrieter, *The New Catholicity: Theology Between the Global and the Local* (New York, 1997).
3   *op. cit.*
4   I am sure that that is a quote from someone, but I cannot remember from whom!
5   *Lettres et Messages d'Algerie* (Paris, 1996).
6   *Who are we Now? Christian Humanism and the Global Market from Hegel to Heaney* (Edinburgh, 1998, p. 120).
7   Aidan Nichols OP, *The Word has Been Abroad* (Edinburgh, 1998, p.1).
8   Quoted by R. Harries, *Art and the Beauty of God: A Christian Understanding* (London, 1993, p. 4).
9   Quoted by S. Hauerwas, *Santify Them in the Truth* (Edinburgh, 1998, p. 38).
10 Neil MacGregor, *Seeing Salvation* (BBC London, 2000, p. 49).
11 Hans Kessler, 'Fulfilment: experienced for a moment yet painfully lacking?' *Concilium* (September 1999, 103).
12 Cf. Alberto Moreira, 'The dangerous memory of Jesus Christ in a post-traditional society', and Ferdinand D. Dagmang 'Gratification and instantaneous liberation', both in *Concilium* (September 1999).
13 *The Theology of Grace* (Dublin, 1974, p. 74f.).
14 *Ibid.*, p.166.
15 *Open to Judgment.* (London, 1996, p. 268f.).
16 Meister Eckhart, *Sermons and Treatises*, Vol. II (London, 1981, p.14).
17 *Ibid.*, p. 23f.

To Praise, to Bless, To Preach: The Mission of the Dominican Family[1]

When I was asked to address this Assembly of the Dominican Family, I was extremely excited. I am convinced that if we can come to share a common preaching of the gospel, then it will renew the whole Order. But I also felt very inadequate. Who am I to articulate a vision of that common mission? How can any individual friar, sister, nun or lay Dominican do this? It is together, listening to each other, that we need to discover that new vision, and that is why we are here in Manila. So I thought that what I should do is to listen with you to the Word of God. All preaching begins with listening to the gospel. Since we are preachers of the Resurrection, the text that I have chosen is of the Risen Christ appearing to the disciples in John's Gospel.

> On the evening of that day, the first day of the week, the doors being shut where the disciples were, for fear of the Jews, Jesus came and stood among them and said to them, 'Peace be with you.' And he showed them his hands and his side. Then the disciples were glad when they saw the Lord. Jesus said to them again, 'Peace be with you. As the Father has sent me, so I send you.' And when he had said this, he breathed on them, and said to them, 'Receive the Holy Spirit. If you forgive the sins of any, they are forgiven; if you retain the sins of any, they are retained.' (John 20: 19–23)

That scene of the disciples seems very far away from this meeting of the Dominican Family. There you have a little group of disciples, locked away in the upper room, not daring to go out because they are afraid. And here we are, 9000 kilometres away and almost 2000 years later, in this great meeting hall. They were a little group of Jews, and we in this meeting are 160 people from 58 nationalities, with our brothers and sisters from the Dominican Family in the Philippines. They did not dare to leave the room, but we have come from all over the planet.

And yet in many ways, we are just like them. Their story is our story. We, too, are locked in our own little rooms; we, too, have our fears which imprison us. The Risen Christ also comes to us to open the doors, and send us on the way. We, too, will discover who we are as a Dominican Family, and what is our mission, not by gazing at ourselves, but in meeting the Risen Lord. He also says to us: 'Peace be with you', and sends us to preach forgiveness and reconciliation. And that is why I wish to reflect on this story and discover what it says about our common mission. It may seem absurd to compare the renewal of the Dominican Family with the resurrection of the dead. But for Christians, all new life is always a sharing in that victory. Paul calls us to die and rise with Christ every day. Even the smallest defeats and victories are shaped by those three days, from Good Friday to Easter Sunday.

On the evening of that day, the first day of the week, the doors being shut where the disciples were, for fear of the Jews ...

The disciples are locked in the upper room. It is a time of waiting, between two lives. The women claim to have met the Risen Lord, but the men have not seen him. As usual, the men are a bit slow! They have seen only an empty tomb, but what does that mean? Their old life with Jesus is over, when they walked with him to Jerusalem, listened to his parables and shared his life. But the new life after the Resurrection has not yet begun. They have heard that Jesus is risen, but have not seen him face to face. And so they wait, or go back to what they were doing before, fishing for fish. It is a moment of transition.

In a small way, the Dominican Family is living such a moment. From the beginning, Dominic gathered together a family of preachers, men and women, lay and religious, contemplatives and preachers who took to the road. In Santa Sabina there are early inscriptions that mention the Dominican Family. It has always been part of who we are. But now we claim that something new is happening. All over the world, sisters and lay Dominicans are claiming their identity as preachers. When we read the Acts of General Chapters of the brethren, we are told that this is a new moment in our history. We proclaim that all the members of the Dominican Family are equal and that we share a common mission. There are lots of beautiful documents. But some of us are like the disciples. We have not seen much evidence of change as yet. Most things seem to go on much as before. We hear wonderful stories of a new collaboration, but it usually appears to be happening somewhere else, and not where we are! So, we may be like the disciples in the upper room; waiting, hopeful but uncertain.

This is part of the experience of the whole Church at the moment. We have beautiful documents from the Second Vatican Council proclaiming the dignity of the lay vocation. We have statements about the place of women in the life and mission of the Church. We have a new vision of the Church, as the pilgrim people of God. But sometimes we may feel that nothing much seems to have changed. In fact, sometimes the Church seems even more clerical than it was before. And so for many Catholics this is a time of mixed feelings: of hope and disappointment, of renewal and frustration, of joy and anger.

And then there is fear. The disciples are locked up in their upper room by fear. Of what are we afraid? What fears keep us locked inside some little space, reluctant to try something new? We must dare to see the fears that lock us in and prevent us from throwing ourselves wholeheartedly into the mission of the Dominican Family. Maybe we are afraid of losing the distinctive tradition of our congregation with its own founder, its unique history and stories. Maybe we are afraid that we will try something new and fail. Sometimes the brethren are nervous about working with women, even their sisters! Sometimes the sisters are nervous of working with men, even their brothers! It is safer just to carry on doing what we have always done. Let's go on fishing for fish.

Jesus came and stood among them and said to them, 'Peace be with you.' And he showed them his hands and his side. Then the disciples were glad when they saw the Lord.

It is the sight of the wounded Christ that frees the disciples from fear and makes them glad. It is the wounded Christ that transforms them into preachers.

One cannot be a preacher without getting wounded. The Word became flesh, and was hurt and killed. He was powerless in the face of the powers of this world. He dared to be vulnerable to what they might do to him. If we are preachers of that same Word, then we will also get hurt. At the heart of the preaching of St Catherine of Siena was her vision of the wounded Christ, and she was given a share of his wounds. We may only suffer small wounds; being mocked, or not taken seriously. We may be tortured, like our brother Tito de Alencar in Brazil, or killed, like Pierre Claverie in Algeria and Joaquin Bernardo in Albania, and our four sisters in Zimbabwe in the 1970s. The vision of the wounded but living Christ can free us from the fear of getting wounded. We can take the risk because hurt and death do not have the victory.

When we see that wounded Christ, then we can face the fact that we are *already* hurt. Perhaps we have been hurt by our childhood, by growing up in dysfunctional families or by our experience of religious life, by botched attempts to love, by ideological conflicts in the Church, by sin. Every one of us is a wounded preacher. But the good news is that we are preachers *because* we are wounded. Gerald Vann, an English Dominican, was one of the most famous writers on spirituality in the English-speaking world since the Second World War. He struggled with alcoholism and depression all his life. That is why he had something to say. We have a word of hope and mercy because we have needed them ourselves. On my bookshelves I have a book written by an old French Dominican called *Les Cicatrices*, ('The Scars'). In this book he tells how he came to Christ through the hurts of his life. And when he gave it to me he wrote a dedication saying, 'For Timothy, who knows that the scars can become the doors of the sun.' Every wound we have can become a door for the rising sun. One brother suggested that I should show you my wounds. I am afraid that you will have to wait for my memoirs!

The most painful thing for the disciples is that they look at the Jesus whom *they* have wounded. They denied him, deserted him, ran away. They hurt him. Jesus does not accuse them; he just shows them his wounds. We must face the fact that we too have wounded each other. So often I have seen the brethren wound other members of the Dominican Family unintentionally, through a patronizing word or by a failure to treat women or lay people as our equals. But it is not only the brothers. We all have the power to hurt; the power to speak words that wound, the power of the priests over the laity, of men over women and of women over men, of religious over laity, of superiors over the members of their community, of the rich over the poor, of the confident over the fearful.

We can dare to see the wounds that we have inflicted and received, and still be glad, because Christ is risen from the dead. We may hobble on one foot, but the Lord makes us happy. This was Dominic's joy, and there is no preaching of the good news without it. Earlier this year, a team from French TV came to spend a few days at Santa Sabina to make a programme. At the end the director said to me, 'It is very strange. In this community you talk about serious things, and yet you are all always laughing.' We are joyful wounded preachers.

Jesus said to them again, 'Peace be with you. As the Father has sent me, so I send you.'

Jesus sends the disciples out of the safety of the locked room. This sending is the beginning of the preaching. To be a preacher is to be sent by God, but we are not all sent in the same way. For the sisters and the brothers this will often mean, literally, being sent to another place. My brethren sent me to Rome. It is my hope that, with the evolution of the Volunteer movement, we will see lay people being sent to other parts of the world to share in our preaching; Bolivians to the Philippines, and Filipinos to France. For many of us, being sent means that we must be prepared to pack our bags and go. I remember an old friar telling me that no brother should possess more than he can carry in his two hands. How many of us could do that?

But for many members of the Dominican family being sent does not mean travel. The nuns are members of the monastery, and usually that is where they will stay all of their lives. Many lay

Dominicans are married or have jobs, which means that they cannot just get up and go. So being sent means more than physical mobility. It means being from God. It is our being. Jesus is 'the one who is sent' (Hebrews 3:1). He is sent from the Father, but that did not mean that Jesus left heaven and came to another place called earth. His very existence is to be from the Father. Being sent is who he is, now and for ever!

Being a preacher means that every one of us is sent from God to those whom we meet. The wife is sent to the husband and the husband to the wife. Each is a word of God to the other. The nun may not be able to leave her monastery, but she is just as much sent as any brother. She is sent to her sisters, and the whole monastery is a word of God sent to us. Sometimes we accept our mission by remaining where we are and being a word of life there.

One of my favourite lay fraternities is in Norfolk Prison in Massachusetts, in the United States. The members of that fraternity cannot go elsewhere. If they try they will be stopped forcibly. But they are preachers in that prison, sent to be a word of hope in a place of suffering. They are sent as preachers to a place to which most of us cannot go.

But Jesus does not just send the disciples out of the locked room; he also gathers them into community. He sends them to the ends of the earth, and commands them to be one, as he and the Father are one. They are gathered into community and despatched on mission. I believe that this paradox is central to Dominican life. When Dominic received the bull confirming the Order, he went back to his little community in Toulouse and he dispersed the brethren. No sooner was the community founded than it was broken up. The brethren were not at all keen to go, but, for once, Dominic insisted.

For Dominic, the Order disperses the brethren and gathers them into unity. We are sent away to preach, but we are one because we preach the one Kingdom, into which all of humanity is called. As Paul writes, we preach 'one body and one Spirit, just as you were called to the one hope that belongs to your call, one Lord, one faith, one baptism, one God and Father of us all' (Ephesians 4:4). We cannot preach the Kingdom and be divided. This is why we have always struggled not to split into separate orders. Sometimes, we only hung on by the skin of our teeth!

So, for the brethren, from the beginning this has been the pulse of our lives; being sent out and gathered back into unity. It is the breathing of the Order; and the genius of Dominic was to give this breathing strong lungs, which are our democratic form of government. Government is not just a form of administration; it embodies a spirituality of mission; it is the lungs that breathe us out on mission, and suck us back into community. In the early centuries there was a General Chapter every year. Every year the brethren gathered in Bologna or Paris, and set out on new missions. All year long there were brethren on the road, walking to Bologna or Paris to meet for the Chapter, and then walking away to new exotic places of mission, like England!

Dominican Family has different ways of being sent. How are we to be one? What form will our communion take? What are our lungs that breathe us out and draw us together again? We are just at the beginning of reflecting on this. The monasteries of nuns feel deeply part of the one Order, and yet each monastery has its own precious autonomy. For many branches of the Family unity has never been so important. Many congregations of sisters came into existence through a process of splitting, dividing like cells. Juridical unity was not important for our sisters. With Dominican Sisters International, the sisters are at the beginning of discovering how 160 congregations can collaborate together and find unity. As yet, there is no worldwide structure which brings together the Dominican laity.

I believe that we must start by finding our unity in the mission. We are sent out together to preach the one Kingdom, in which all humanity is reconciled. Our unity with each other will be discovered as we go out together. We will need new structures to build a common mission. Already these are beginning to emerge. The Bologna General Chapter, two years ago, encouraged the Dominican family who live in the same place to meet and plan a common mission. In Mexico City or Paris, for example, the whole Family can meet to decide what is our common mission here. At the International level, the General Council of the brethren is meeting regularly with the co-ordinating team of DSI, to share each other's concerns. When we found the Order in new places, we should try, from the beginning, to plan the new presence as an initiative of the whole Dominican Family.

At this meeting our aim is not to set up new juridical structures; we have no authority to do this. In the future we can discover together what structures best serve that unity. Today, we have the far more fundamental and important task of discovering a common vision of the mission. That is the first step to unity. And so let us return to the appearance of the Risen Christ, and see what vision of mission we have here.

Jesus says to the disciples, 'I send you'

He gives the disciples authority to speak. The preacher does not just communicate information; we speak with authority. If we are all to claim our identity as preachers, then we must recognize each other's authority to preach the gospel.

In the first place we all have the authority to preach because we are baptized. This is the clear teaching of the Church, in *Evangelii Nuntiandi, Redemptoris Missio* and *Christifideles Laici*. We have been baptized into the death and resurrection of Christ, and so we must proclaim it. Each of us also has a unique authority because of who we are and the gifts that we have been given. Each of us has a word to proclaim which is given to no-one else. God is in our lives, as married and single people, as parents and as children. Out of these human experiences of love – its triumphs and failures – we have a word to speak of the God who is love. We also have authority because of our skills and knowledge. We are politicians and physicists, cooks and carpenters; we are teachers and taxi drivers, lawyers and economists. I went to a meeting, in Goias, in Brazil, of members of the Dominican Family who are lawyers. They had their special authority as lawyers, to address issues of justice and peace in the continent.

Ultimately, the authority of our preaching is that of the truth, *Veritas*. This is the truth for which human beings are made and which they recognize instinctively. When fray Luis Munio de Zamora OP drew up the first rule for the Dominican fraternities in the thirteenth century, he did not invite them just to be penitents, as was the tradition then; he wanted them to be people of the truth, 'true sons of Dominic in the Lord, filled to the utmost with strong and ardent zeal for Catholic truth, in ways in keeping with their own life'. It is a truth that we must seek together, in places like Aquinas Institute, in St Louis, USA, where lay Dominicans and sisters and brethren study and teach together. Seeking can be painful. It can lead us to be misunderstood and even condemned, like our brother Marie-Joseph Lagrange. But it gives our words authority and it responds to humanity's deepest thirst.

Sister Christine Mwale from Zimbabwe has spoken here of the cooking-pot around which the African family gathers. This pot rests on three stones, which she has compared with the three forms of authority in the Dominican Family: the authority we have as individuals; the delegated authority of the elders; and the authority of the group. If we are to be truly a family of preachers, then we must recognize each other's authority. I must be open to the authority of a sister because she speaks from the truth of her experience as a woman; also perhaps as a teacher, or a theologian. I must give authority to the lay Dominican who knows more than I do about so many things; perhaps marriage, or some science or skill. If we recognize each other's authority then we will be truly a family of preachers. Together we can find an authority which none of us has individually. We must find our voice together.

For many Dominicans, the discovery that we all have the authority to preach has been exciting and liberating. And the exclusion of the non-ordained from preaching after the gospel during the Eucharist is deeply painful for many. It is experienced as a negation of their full identity as preachers.

All that I can say is this: do not be discouraged. Accept every occasion to preach. Let us together create new occasions. Whether we agree or disagree with this ruling, it is not for us the crux of the matter. Preaching in a pulpit has always been only a small part of our preaching. In fact, one could argue that Dominic wished to carry the preaching of the gospel out of the confines of the Church and into the street. He wished to carry the Word of God to where people are, living and studying, and arguing and relaxing. For us, the challenge is to preach in new places, on the Internet, through art, in a thousand ways. It would be paradoxical if we thought that preaching in the pulpit was the only real way of proclaiming the gospel. It would be a form of fundamentalism that would go against the creativity of Dominic, a retreat back into the church.

I know that this might look like an evasion, an excuse for depriving lay people and sisters of active preaching of the Word in the ordinary sense of the word. It could look as if we are saying that the non-ordained should settle for a lesser form of preaching. But this is not so. The Order of Preachers exists to go out and share the good news, especially to those who do not come to us. We do this in an incredible variety of ways: writing books, appearing on the television, visiting the sick. However, much the exclusion from the pulpit may be hurtful and not accepted, I do not believe that it is the big issue.

We are all 'good stewards of God's varied grace' (1 Peter 4:10) in different ways. Each of us has received the *gratia predicationis*, but differently. The Dominican martyrs in Vietnam, China and Japan in the seventeenth century were men and women, lay and religious, with an extraordinary diversity of ways of being a preacher. St Dominic Uy was a Vietnamese Dominican layman who was known as 'The Master Preacher', and so, obviously, he proclaimed the word; Peter Ching was a Chinese layman who took part in public debates in Fogan to defend the truth of Christianity, just like Dominic with the Albigensians. But other lay Dominicans who were martyred were catechists, inn-keepers, merchants and scholars.

We preach the Word which has become flesh, and that Word of God can become flesh in all that we are, and not just in what we say. St Francis of Assisi said: 'Preach the gospel at all times. If necessary use words!' We have to become living words of truth and hope. St Paul wrote to the Corinthians, 'You are a letter from Christ delivered by us, written not with ink but with the Spirit of the living God, not on tablets of stone, but on the tablets of the human heart' (2 Cor 3:3). In some situations the most effective word can even be silence. I was struck in Japan by how our monasteries are powerful witnesses to the gospel. Buddhists may meet Christ more powerfully in the silence of the nuns than in any words that we could say. I think of the lepers' colonies here in the Philippines, run by the brothers of St Martin, which are an embodiment of Dominic's compassion. The Word also becomes visible in poetry and painting, in music and dancing. Every skill gives us a way of propagating the Word. For example, Hilary Pepler, a famous lay Dominican and a printer, wrote that

> The work of the printer, as all work, should be done for the glory of God. The work of the printer is to multiply the written word, hence the printer serves the maker of words, and the maker of words serves – or should serve – the Word which becomes Flesh.[2]

We do not preach this Word as scattered individuals, but as a community. *Christifideles Laici* says that communion with Jesus 'gives rise to communion of Christians among themselves ... Communion gives rise to mission and mission is accomplished in communion' (n. 32). As you all know, in the early days a community of the brethren was known as a *sacra praedicatio*, a holy preaching. When Antonio de Montesinos preached his famous sermon in defence of the Indians in Hispaniola, in 1511, the Spanish Conquistadors went to complain to the prior, Pedro de Cordoba, and the prior told them that when Antonio preached the whole community preached. We should be midwives to each other, helping our sisters and brothers to speak the Word that is given to them. We must help each other to find the authority that is given to them. Together we are a living Word in a way that we could not be separately.

I met a brother in the United States recently who had had an operation for cancer and lost part of his tongue. He had to learn to speak again. He discovered how complex it is to speak a single word. We need parts of the body we never think of: our minds, lungs, throat, vocal cords, tongue, teeth and mouth. All this is necessary just to say: 'Peace be with you'. And if we are to proclaim this to the world, then we need each other so that we can together form these words of life. Together we are the mind, the lungs, the tongue, the mouth, the teeth, the vocal cords that can form a word of peace.

I was at a meeting of the Dominican Family in Bologna earlier this year. Here Dominic is buried, but here his family is alive. There is a group of laity who work with the sisters and brethren in preaching missions in parishes. There is another group of laity and brethren whose love is philosophy, and who saw their mission as confronting the intellectual vacuum at the heart of people's lives. They preach by teaching. And there was a group of sisters who ran a university for the retired and unemployed. And there was a fraternity of laity who said that they wished to support the mission of the others by praying. There was no competition between these Dominicans.

No group could claim to be the 'true Dominicans' or that the others are 'second-class citizens'. There can be no competition between the nuns and the sisters as to who is more Dominican. The lay fraternities have been a vital part of the Dominican Order since the beginning and remain so today. It is true that there are many new lay groups. Like new-born babies, they may need more care and be the focus of more attention, but they in no way challenge the position of the fraternities at the heart of the life of the Order. There can be no competition between us. If there is then we will fail to embody the gospel.

And when he had said this, he breathed on them, and said to them, 'Receive the Holy Spirit'

Jesus breathes upon the disciples. This echoes the creation of humanity, when God breathed upon Adam and made him a living being. Jesus breathes on the disciples so that they become fully alive. This is the completion of creation. Peter says to Jesus, 'You have the words of eternal life' (John 6: 68). The goal of preaching is not to communicate information but life. The Lord says to Ezekiel, 'Thus says the Lord God to these bones: Behold, I will cause breath to enter you, and you shall live' (37:5f.) We preachers should speak words that make dry bones come alive!

We must be honest and admit that most preaching is very boring, and is more inclined to put us to sleep than to wake us up. At least it drives us to prayer. After ten minutes we discreetly look at our watches and pray for the preacher to stop. The Colombian Dominicans say: 'Five minutes for the people, five minutes for the walls, and everything else is for the Devil.' Even Paul, the greatest of all preachers, managed to send Eutychus to sleep, so that he fell out of the window and almost died! But God sometimes gives us the grace to speak words that give life.

I met a woman here in the Philippines called Clarentia. She had caught leprosy when she was fourteen years old, and spent all of her life in leprosaria, living with our Brothers of St Martin. She hardly dared to leave these places where she was accepted and welcomed. Now that she is already in her sixties, she has discovered her vocation as a preacher; she has found the courage to leave her locked 'upper room', to go out and to visit leprosaria to encourage the people who are there also to find a freedom; she addresses conferences and government agencies. She has found her voice and authority. This is what it means to preach a word of life.

For us preachers, all words matter. All our words can offer life to other people, or death. The vocation of all members of the Dominican Family is to offer words that give life. All day long we are offering words to each other; we joke and tease, we exchange information, we gossip, we repeat the news, and talk about the people who are not in the room. Do these words offer life or death, healing or hurt? A computer virus was sent out from this city, Manila, earlier this year. It was disguised in a message called 'I LOVE YOU'. But if that message was opened, then all your computer files were destroyed. Sometimes our words can be similar. We can give the impression that we are just being truthful, just or honest, 'I am just saying this for your own good, my dear', while sowing poison!

One motto of the Order is *Laudare, benedicere, praedicare* ('to praise, to bless, to preach'). Becoming a preacher is more than learning to speak about God. It is discovering the art of praising and blessing all that is good. There is no preaching without celebration. We cannot preach unless we celebrate and praise the goodness of what God has made. Sometimes the preacher must, like Las Casas, confront and denounce injustice, but only so that life may have the victory over death, and resurrection over the tomb, and praise over accusation.

We will, therefore, only flourish as a family of preachers if we make each other strong and give each other life. We must breathe God's breath into each other, as Jesus did on the disciples. St Catherine of Siena was a preacher not just in what she said and wrote, but in giving others strength. When the Pope was getting discouraged, she stiffened his courage. When her beloved Raymond of Capua, the Master of the Order, was afraid, then she encouraged him onwards. All Masters of the Order need that sometimes! When a criminal was condemned to death, she helped him to face execution. She says to him, 'Courage, my dear brother, we shall soon be at the wedding feast . . . Never forget this. I shall be waiting for you at the place of execution.'[3]

The Dominican Family in Brazil established what is called 'The Dominican mutirão'. Mutirão means 'working together'. Every year a small group of brethren, sisters and laity goes to be with people struggling for life or justice, especially those who are poor and forgotten. They go just to be with them, to show support, to hear what they are enduring, to show that someone remembers them. We need this if we are to be strong.

Most of us learnt to be strong and human in our families. Our parents and siblings, aunts and uncles and cousins, taught us how to talk and listen, how to play and laugh, how to walk and get up when we fall over. You cannot learn to be human alone. Perhaps this is

why we have always thought of the Order as a family, with nuns and
laity and brethren. Dominic was eminently human and he preached
the God who embraced our humanity. We need our Dominican
Family to form us human preachers, who can rejoice in the God
who shares our humanity. We need the wisdom of women, and the
experience of married people and parents, and the depth of
contemplatives if we are to be formed as human preachers.

So all Dominican formation should be mutual formation. In
many parts of the world, the novices of the sisters and the brothers
spend part of their formation together. Often we drastically
underestimate how much our lay Dominicans can teach the other
branches of the Dominican Family. You have a wisdom to which
we are not always attentive. Conversely, in many parts of the world,
lay Dominicans are thirsting for a full formation in the theology and
spirituality of the Order which we do not always offer. This is surely
one of the most urgent priorities now. How can we respond?

And the last words of Jesus that I will comment upon show us
what is at the heart of that word of life.

'If you forgive the sins of any, they are forgiven; if you retain the sins of any, they are retained'

Twice Jesus says to them, 'Peace be with you', and then he gives
them the power to forgive or retain sins. That is the heart of our
preaching. During this Assembly, there has emerged a particular
stress on the commitment to justice and peace as a major focus for
our common mission as a Dominican Family. I think, for example,
of Dominican Peace Action in Britain, a group of nuns, sisters, laity
and brethren who make a commitment to work together for peace
and especially the abolition of nuclear weapons, through writing and
preaching, and even through breaking the law.

But the preaching of peace and forgiveness is a vocation that we
may live in many ways. There was a French Dominican lay woman,
called Maïti Girtanner, who was a brilliant young pianist. But in
1940, during the Nazi occupation of France, she founded a
resistance group. Finally, she was caught by the Gestapo and
tortured by a young doctor. This destroyed her nervous system, and
for the rest of her life she was in pain. It destroyed her career as a

pianist. Forty years later, this doctor realized that before he died he had to seek her forgiveness. And so he tracked down Maïti and asked for reconciliation. She forgave him and he returned home, able to face himself, his family and his death. As Maïti said, *Vous voyez le mal n'est pas le plus fort* ('You see, evil is not strongest'). That, too, is an embodiment of Jesus' preaching.

There is a community of brethren in Rome which is entrusted with hearing confessions in the Basilica of Santa Maria Maggiore. For hours every day, especially during this Jubilee year, and in innumerable languages, they are there to offer God's forgiveness. All these are ways of preaching those words, 'Peace be with you'. But we cannot preach that peace unless we live it among ourselves. When the brethren and sisters make profession they ask for God's mercy and that of the Order. We can have nothing to say about peace and forgiveness if we do not offer it to each other.

When war broke out between Argentina and Britain over the Malvinas Islands in 1982, the brethren of the community in Oxford went out into the street in the habit and carrying candles. We went in procession to the war memorial to pray for peace. Last year I happened to be in Argentina on Malvinas Day, the day when the nation renews its commitment to the islands. I was in Tucuman in the north of the country, and the streets were filled with Argentinean flags and banners. I must admit that I wondered whether I had chosen the right day to come! In the afternoon I went to a meeting of a thousand members of the Dominican Family, and there was a little British flag too! And we celebrated the Eucharist together for all the dead, Argentinean and British. The peace we preach is a peace that we must live.

In the north of Burundi, there is a Dominican monastery of nuns. The whole countryside has been destroyed by the violent civil war between the Tutsis and the Hutus. Everywhere the villages are empty and the fields are burnt. But when you draw near to the hill upon which the monastery is built, you see that it is green. Here the people come to tend their fields. In this desert of war it is an oasis of peace. And it is so because the nuns themselves live peacefully together, although they too are Hutu and Tutsi. All of them have lost members of their families in the war. It is a peace and a forgiveness that is made flesh in their community.

This peace that we should share is much more than an absence of conflict. It is more than forgiving each other when we do wrong. It is the friendship that is the heart of Dominican spirituality. Before he died Jesus said to the disciples, 'I call you my friends'. Three days later, after betrayal, denial, suffering and death, he appears among them and offers them again his friendship, 'Peace be with you'. It is a friendship which can transcend any betrayal or cowardice or sin. It is the friendship which is God's own life, the love at the heart of the Trinity.

This friendship is the foundation of our equality with each other. It means that we all equally belong in the Dominican Family. The Dominican Family is our common home. We are called to be *chez nous*, in *la nuestra casa*. Sometimes the sisters and laity can feel that in our Dominican home the brethren are in the upper room and they have tried to lock out everyone else. One of our biggest challenges is building a shared consciousness of the Order as the place where we all belong. To be at home means that one does not have to justify being there, that one is at ease. One is accepted just as one is. This shows in our faces, gestures and words, in the welcome we give each other. Of course, each community needs its own time and its own space. We cannot all go barging into the monasteries and demanding to share the lives of the nuns. The communities of brethren and sisters and the families of the laity need their own privacy.

Many little tensions within the Dominican Family, such as who can put which initials after their names, who can wear the habit and when, are symptoms of this more important and deeper longing, for friendship, for a home, to belong, to have one's assured place at the table or around the cooking-pot. In the past we used to belong to the First, Second and Third Order. This terminology was abolished at the General Chapter of River Forest in 1968, to make plain our equality. No-one is first or second or third class. But in so doing we lost a way of stating our unity in a common Order. Together we must find ways to build that common home.

And it should be an open home, which welcomes the friends of our friends, which welcomes new groups whose Dominican identity is not, perhaps, clear but who want to be part of the Family. The friendship that Jesus offers is wide and open. He welcomes in everyone. He gets impatient when the disciples try to stop someone preaching because they do not belong to the group of the disciples. He does not shut doors but bursts through them. Let us embody that big-hearted friendship, Dominic's magnanimity. Let us be a sign of that welcome, so that we may all be at ease in Dominic's Family. May Dominic liberate us from the fear that locks the doors.

1   The keynote address to the first ever meeting of all branches of the Dominican Family: nuns, active sisters, friars and laity. It took place in Manila, The Philippines, in October 2000, with the aim of developing a common mission of preaching for the whole Dominican family.
2   Aidan Nichols OP (ed.) *Dominican Gallery* (Leominster, 1997, p. 347).
3   L. 273; DT XXXI.

The Challenge of Europe

Note: Lecture given in Prague in 1993 to a meeting of the European Provincials of the Order.

I have been asked to talk about the challenges facing the Order in Europe. And I think that it is good that we are addressing this question here in Prague, because it is a city certainly in the heart of Europe. Karl Jaspers once said that Europe stretched from San Francisco to Vladivostok, which is over-inclusive. George Steiner, who teaches in Geneva and Cambridge, said that Europe runs from Lisbon to St Petersburg, thus leaving out not only Moscow but also England and Ireland. This reminds me of De Gaulle, who was once asked who were the greatest European authors, and he replied, 'Dante, Goethe and Chateaubriand, mon General, not Shakespeare. You asked me about Europe.' But here in Prague we are certainly in Europe, and it is perhaps here that some of the basic questions are being asked.

Truth speaking

Vaclav Havel, the President of the new Czech Republic, has often said that the real challenge of the moment is to speak truthfully. The threat to our civilization is, perhaps, not just that we speak untruthfully, that we tell lies, but that we speak easily words that have become empty. He analysed, in a famous essay, the case of the greengrocer who hangs in his window the slogan 'Workers of the World Unite'.

In some ways that it is also our challenge in the Church; to speak words that actually mean something, that have weight and authority. I was in a church in Rome recently, listening to a sermon. All that the priest said was good. He told us of the need for justice and peace, he told us to love one another, to build the Church as a community and so on. No-one could object to what he said. But as I looked at the faces of the congregation, especially the young, I could see that they did not believe him. The words meant nothing. They were just words. They were like the words of the scribes and the pharisees, not like those of Jesus who spoke with authority. How should we live so that we may speak with authority, as preachers should do?

I think that this was a challenge of which we became acutely aware in Mexico at the General Chapter. Many of us felt that we did not need many more documents, many more statements of 'vision'. The last general chapters had helped us to formulate a vision. We have the four priorities of the Order and the five frontiers and so on. And these are good and right and important. The challenge of this moment was not to produce yet more documents, but to wonder how we might incarnate that vision, make it flesh and blood, so that we could speak with authority. I think that that is a challenge of the next Chapter at Caleruega.

Let me give you just a little example. For many years in England I was involved in campaigning against war, against nuclear war, war in the Falklands, war in the Gulf. I spoke many, many words about war. But in Africa recently I saw war, and it reduced me to silence. I went to the war zone in Rwanda to see the work of our sisters; I went to a refugee camp with 35,000 people and saw children who had given up trying to live. I went to a hospital with wards filled with young men and children who had no legs, because they had been blown off by mines. We saw and we could say almost nothing. At the end of the day we did the only thing possible, which was to celebrate the Eucharist together. Here was a memory which made it possible to endure what we had seen. And whatever words we could say then would be at the other side of that silence.

So the first challenge for us as an Order in this new Europe that is emerging is not, perhaps, what to say, but how to speak. How should we live that we may speak with authority, and not like the scribes and the Pharisees?

And I would like to suggest four specific challenges. There are many more, but I do not want to speak for too long:

(a) In a world which distrusts anyone who wishes to teach, how are

we to be preachers and teachers?
(b) In a world of consumerism, how are we to be poor?
(c) In a world which tends to fatalism, how are we to be free?
(d) In a world of migration, of refugees and immigrants, how are we to be welcoming?

Each of them presents specific and concrete challenges to us as Dominicans, as to how we live the religious life.

In a world which distrusts anyone who wishes to teach, how are we to be preachers and teachers?

Jesus says, in the last discourse of John's Gospel, 'The word which you hear is not mine, but the Father's who sent me' (14:24). To be a preacher, to speak a word of authority, is to speak words that we have been given, that are not our own. We speak what has been revealed.

How can we preach in a society which is profoundly distrustful of any conception of revelation? In our society the only authentic word is that which you speak from yourself, out of your own experience. It is a society which both longs for teaching, and yet which is deeply suspicious of it, especially if it comes from the Church. So our first challenge is this: How can we be an Order of teachers when the very idea of teaching anyone anything is suspected as an act of imposition?

An English theologian, the first Catholic professor of theology at Cambridge since the Reformation, described the crisis like this:

> The legacy of the Enlightenment left us with what we might call a crisis of docility. Unless we have the courage to work things out for ourselves, to take as true only that which we have personally ascertained or, perhaps, invented, then meanings and values, descriptions and instructions, imposed by other people, feeding other people's power, will inhibit and enslave us, bind us into fables and falsehoods from the past. Even God's truth, perhaps especially God's truth, is no exception to this rule. Only slaves and children should be teachable or docile.[1]

We could speculate for hours about the roots of this crisis. I suspect that it lies in a wedge driven at the time of the Enlightenment between the activity of thinking on the one hand and tradition on the other. The Enlightenment posited a fundamental opposition between them. The thinking man, the enlightened person, was the one who thought for himself, who accepted nothing on trust, whose first instinct was always to doubt. The tradition, especially of the Church, was the symbol of intolerance, prejudice and the failure to think for oneself. This puts into doubt the role of the teacher or preacher.

It is often said that the crisis of the faith in Europe is that of secularization. I think that this is too simple an analysis. There remains a deep hunger for God, and a yearning for revelation. People long to be told what is the meaning of their lives, as long as it is by anyone other than a Christian teacher. The shops are filled with books about the occult, witchcraft, astrology, visitors from outer space, eastern religion. But this hunger for knowledge is divorced from the process of thinking, arguing, speculating. Seeking and finding, invention and discovery, have become divorced from each other, and our own beloved theology threatens to drop into the hole in the middle. For at the heart of our tradition is the belief that it is in seeking that we discover, and it is in struggling to understand that we meet the God who gives himself.

I think that we must realize that this is a split which runs deeply within the Church itself. We are all children of the Enlightenment, and so our culture pushes us towards scepticism or fundamentalism, scriptural or doctrinal. Divisions within provinces and within our theological institutions reflect these two ways of looking at the world. There is a crisis of the role of thinking within theology, as there is within the whole culture.

I would say that one of the fundamental challenges of the Order is to teach people how to see that thinking belongs to our reception of God's revelation. Argument and disagreement, disputation and debate, are part of the way in which we lovingly accept the truth that God gives to us.

In the Church today there is much fear. And much of that fear is a fear of thinking, a fear of disagreement. I think that we must form Dominicans who have no fear of argument because that belongs to drawing near to the mystery. St Thomas was a theologian who always started with the objections of his opponents, objections which he took seriously. And this was not because he wanted to show why they were wrong, but to show in what limited sense they were right. The whole medieval *disputatio* was a debate through which you tried to learn from your opponent. St Thomas was a mendicant scholar, one who begged for the truth. He was like Jacob wrestling with the angel, so that he might demand his benediction.

I would say that a fundamental challenge, if we are to be preachers, is to heal the rift between thought and belief. Our theological centres – the Angelicum, Salamanca, Fribourg, Manilla – should be known as places in which the brethren have the courage to debate the issues of the day without fear, where we disagree with each other so as to learn. Disagreement should be our specialty *de la maison*!

This is a challenge which I see in Fribourg, for example, where there is a fierce argument over the nature of our presence in the theology faculty; this is the challenge in the Angelicum, where I spent a week recently. And I would say that there is much more openness than I had dreamt of for facing this. In a Church in which theological dialogue is afflicted with clichés, like a child covered with measles, this is surely what we have to be known for. Do we dare in our Provinces to let surface the differences that divide us, so that we may debate them without fear?

And maybe here, Prague, is a particularly good place to face this challenge, because, maybe in central Europe more than some other places, thinking remains a valued and even popular activity, rather than the property of an elite. Culture is not just for those who can afford expensive opera seats. It is for everyone. This is symbolized by the fact that in Bulgaria they even have a Feast of the Alphabet, 24 May, to celebrate the gift of the alphabet by Cyril and Methodius. All the children go around wearing the letters of the alphabet! It is perhaps symbolic of modern Europe that England elected an accountant to be its new Prime Minister but Czechoslovakia, as it then was, a playwright and thinker. And Vaclav Havel wrote recently, 'The era of ideologies seems to have come to an end. I think that we are entering an era of thinking now.'[2] This may be a bit optimistic, but let us hope not. We must see that this is so in the Church too.

A word of grace

I said that it would be too simple to describe our age simply in terms of secularism. There is a deep, and sometimes odd, hunger for religion. Some people try to read the stars. Others, like the Prince of Wales, talk to their plants. Books on the occult fill the shops. Yet it is also true to say that, for enormous numbers of people, perhaps more than in any other culture in the history of the world, God is simply absent. God is not there. The world is not touched by signs of transcendence. When I arrived in Nigeria I was struck by how all-pervasive is religion. Every shop has a religious name: 'God's Power Electrical Equipment', 'The Gospel Haircutting Shop'. The language of preaching has a natural continuity with all other language, because the name of God is never far from anyone's lips. In our culture preaching has become an altogether different activity, because in most of Europe the name of God is not mentioned in public discourse much. How can we begin to preach when the word 'God' is alien to the language of many of our hearers?

This is a favourite topic of mine and so I must resist the temptation to speak much. I would merely say that the dominant culture of the west, and increasingly of the whole world, is that of the market. Our ancestors lived in a world in which markets were important. Our world *is* a market, and all human, economic and political life is subservient to the market. It is the basis of political decisions; it mediates our perception of reality. Everything is for sale and we are all consumers.

The other day, in England, I went to catch a train and I heard an announcement which said that 'consumers should go to platform 8 for the train to Portsmouth'. It sounded as if we were expected to eat the train!

Thirty years ago a man called Polanyi wrote a book in which he argued that the birth of the modern epoch really came with the diffusion of what he called 'the commodity fiction'. Specifically, he examines how land and labour became turned into commodities, things to be bought and sold. Human lives and the natural world became functions of the market, something that would have been unimaginable in the time of St Dominic, for example.

In such a world everything will be seen as merely objects to be bought and sold. Everything will have a price. In such a world God, the giver of all good things, will become hard to see. It will be hard to spot the signs of the presence of God, who is utter gift, when all his gifts have been reduced to goods. If you see your neighbour as just another consumer, then it is hard to see him or her as the child of God, made in the creator's image.

This is a culture, with an implicit atheism, that is rapidly spreading everywhere. I heard a couple of weeks ago how Vilnius, in Lithuania, is quickly being transformed into a western shopping centre, as western and Japanese companies buy up the shops. Our preaching in a Europe in which the east enters into the world market has a particular challenge to face.

How can we possibly preach to this world with words of authority? I find this one of the hardest questions to answer. I can only imagine that it means that we must rediscover the radical freedom of poverty. And what that means I am not at all sure. If we are to talk of the God of gift, then our communities must be islands of an alternative culture, in which we are really free of the seductions of consumerism. And how can that be, when it saturates every aspect of our language, unless we learn how to be radically poor? I hate the very prospect! I cannot see how we can really be preachers in this world, in which everything is for sale and everything has a price, unless we rediscover a marginality. And my impression is that, for all we talk about 'options for the poor', our lifestyles, the way we dress, the holidays that we have, the way that we have time off, is more like those of our contemporaries than it used to be. At a recent meeting of Religious Superiors in Ireland, we talked of the spread in religious communities of the 'fat-cat' culture. I was drawn to the Order, like so many others, by a deep desire for poverty. Has the Order helped to sustain and live that dream?

A word that liberates

This brings me to the third basic challenge that we have to face. As preachers we need to preach a word of truth and not of clichés; a word of grace and not of the market. We need also to preach a word that liberates. We need to speak a word that sets people free. And that is profoundly difficult since our culture is marked by a profound fatalism, a deep belief that nothing can really change. Or if it does ever change then it will not be because of any decisions that we make!

Writing before the fall of the Berlin Wall, Havel said that a characteristic of Soviet Bloc countries was a terrible passivity, a disbelief that anything that anyone did could really make a difference. We are all part of the system. Of course, soon afterwards the whole of central and eastern Europe was shaken by a revolution that took us all by surprise. Things *can* change. But Havel rightly insists that the fatalism of eastern Europe, in fact, was just a mirror of a more fundamental malaise, from which we all suffer, and which he describes as 'the general inability of modern humanity to be the master of its own situation'.[3] Our technological culture, the culture of the market which now dominates the whole world, is deeply marked by fatalism. It is a fatalism that challenges us when we would speak a liberating and transforming word. The so-called 'free world' is marked a by a deep un-freedom.

Last year I toured Africa for two months, and I was confronted with not only war but also a sense everywhere of a collapsing economy, of societies which seemed doomed to move into ever greater poverty and conflict. Almost nowhere did I sense a hope that this process of collapse could be reversed. It seemed to be experienced as an inescapable fate. They were caught in a world economy that made the rich countries richer and the poor poorer. And then I returned to England for a few nights. A ten-year old child had been murdered in Liverpool, and it seemed that this murder had been committed by two other children. There was a sense of deep horror, that this symbolized a social collapse, that society was coming apart. What I also sensed was a feeling that there was little that we could do, that we were being carried towards a doom that we could not avert.

What are the roots of this fatalism, this passivity? How can it be that our society, which has a technological power that has never existed before, can feel so much that our lives are out of our hands? This is not the place to propose an analysis! I could, perhaps, just refer to a recent book that has been very influential in the Anglo-Saxon world. It is called *The Culture of Contentment*, by the most famous American economist John Kenneth Galbraith. And he argues that our politics have been deeply influenced, for the past 200 or so years, by the philosophy of *laissez-faire* (so it is probably the fault of the French!). This asserts that any interference in the market will have a harmful effect. We must let the market work under its principles and all will be alright in the end. This is 'the belief that economic life has within itself the capacity to solve its own problems and for all to work out best in the end'.[4] It is a philosophy that encourages us all to think only in the short term, for, as Keynes said, 'In the long term we are all dead.' The greatest exponent of this philosophy in Britain in recent years was Mrs Thatcher, whose nickname in England was TINA, There Is No Alternative. In the end, what the dominant culture does is to absolve us of responsibility. It consecrates a flight from responsibility.

I think that this is a moment in the history of the Order where we are faced with extraordinary new challenges; for example, the formation of the innumerable young men who wish to join the Order in Africa; the challenge of the evangelization of China; the dialogue with Islam; the re-foundation of the Order in eastern Europe. It is rare that we have had to face such exciting challenges. And we have the men to face them, or rather, if we face them we will have the men. Do we dare take the bold decisions – knowing that we will be blamed and criticized – that will set us free for the challenges of the next century? At the Chapter in Mexico, I appealed for men to help the formation of students in Kinshasa, Zaire, where we have a house of studies with some 40 young men, the future of the Order in Africa. The brethren were excited and came to meetings. Three names were proposed. So far not one has turned up. The Chapter was unable to produce one man for the formation of our young brothers in Africa. Any offers, please see me afterwards!

I think that one of the major challenges for the Order, if we are to live in such a way that we may preach effectively, is to grasp responsibility for the challenges of this moment. Responsibility is the ability to respond. Will we? In my own experience as a Provincial, I have seen 'the mystery of the disappearing responsibility'. It is as mysterious as a Sherlock Holmes novel. A Chapter sees there is a problem and commissions the Provincial to face it and resolve it. A bold decision must be taken. He tells the Provincial Council to consider. The Council appoints a Commission to consider what is to be done. They take two or three years clarifying exactly what is the problem. And they then commit it to the next Provincial Chapter, and so the cycle of irresponsibility continues.

We are the children of our age, and it is to this age that we must preach and make incarnate in our very lives the irrepressible freedom of the children of God. In this historical moment, Havel has written that 'responsibility is our destiny'.[5] If we are to do this as an Order we need to examine the three levels at which mutual responsibility occurs. First of all, within the provinces; do we really have the nerve and the courage to ask Dominicans to sacrifice their own individual desires, their own careers, because of some common projects of the province? Do we have the courage to say to a young friar, 'I know that you want to work in the parish near your old mother, but the province is asking you to go to China'? Then there is the problem of responsibility in co-operation between provinces. In most regions of the world this is now common, especially in areas of common formation. Do we really define where responsibility is to be located, so that difficulties are tackled? I think that this is one of the most urgent problems in the Order. So many inter-provincial projects do not really quite work because no-one is quite sure who is responsible for what.

And the third level of responsibility is for projects that belong to the Order as such. This could be for finding teachers of the Ecole Biblique or finding brethren to work in the new vicariates of eastern Europe, or in just giving the General Council a syndic for the Order! I am finding, as Damian warned me, that it is extremely hard to get people, because often one's natural reaction to any request is to see if there is anyone spare. And usually we do not need the people who are spare! But we must ask the question: Are we a religious order or a federation of provinces?

Now I believe that it is in grasping these practical issues of responsibility that will determine whether we are people of responsibility, people of freedom, who can therefore speak a word that sets free. Or do we succumb to fatalism?

Welcoming the stranger

I cannot resist one final word on yet another challenge which this new Europe presents the Order. And it is that of the strangers in our midst.

The most typically modern society, the USA, consists almost entirely of immigrants, people who have recently moved. Our own Europe is one in which a most fundamental challenge is that of welcoming the stranger, the strangers who come from Morocco to Spain, from the former Soviet Union to Germany, from Algeria to France, from Albania to Italy. Everywhere people are on the move, forced from their homelands by poverty or political persecution. And almost everywhere we can find a new intolerance of the stranger, the *Fremdhass*, the hatred of foreigners in Germany, with the bombing of hostels; the ethnic cleansing in the former Yugoslavia, the conflict of Catholic and Protestant in Northern Ireland, the murder of migrant Algerians in France.

How can we as an Order respond to this challenge? Montesquieu wrote something like this: 'If I knew something that would be useful to myself, but detrimental to my family, I would cast it from my mind. If I knew something that was useful to my family but detrimental to my country I would consider it criminal. If I knew something useful to Europe, but detrimental to humanity I would also consider it a crime'.[6] I find that an interesting text, because it recognizes that we do have identities that are particular. We are born into families and nations, the heirs of particular and unique traditions. And yet it summons us to a larger identity; it invites us to magnanimity. In a Europe marked by immigration, by intolerance, by suspicion of the outsider, we should, above all, as an intentional Order, be those who preserve a magnanimity. And there is a specific challenge.

Many, if not most, European provinces are suffering from shrinking numbers, from pressures of sustaining old commitments, of trying to keep going. The greatest temptation is perhaps to allow ourselves to be forced inward, absorbed by our own provincial problems, surrendering to that fatalism of which I have spoken. Perhaps it is precisely then, when we can least manage it, that we must turn outward and be creative. For me, the most impressive instance of this is the General Vicariate of Belgium. At precisely the moment when it is faced with the collapse of the province and the reduction to a General Vicariate, it takes the option to do something new and something European. At just the moment when it would have been most tempted by introversion it opens up its horizons.

So then, to conclude: in a Europe in which there is a deep hunger for teaching but a distrust of being taught, especially by the Church, we must look to our centres of study. Are they places in which our students really learn to think? Are they places in which the issues of the day, of the Church and the world, are debated without fear? In a Europe seduced by consumerism, in which the God of gift and grace is so often absent, have we the courage to be really poor? In a society which is tempted by fatalism, do we dare to take hard decisions, bear responsibility, and so give some hint of what might be meant by the liberty of the children of God? In a Europe filled with immigrants, do we really communicate a largeness of vision and a magnanimity of heart?

And when one of our brothers talks too much, will we be prepared to forgive him?

1   Nicholas Lash, *Believing Three Ways in One God* (London, 1992, p. 10).
2   *Visions of Europe*, edited by Richard Kearney (Dublin, 1992, p. 129).
3   *Living in Truth* (London, 1986, p. 115).
4   *The Culture of Contentment* (London, 1992, p. 79).
5   *Ibid.*, p. xix.
6   Quoted by Julia Kristeva in *Visions of Europe: Conversations on the Legacy and Future of Europe* (ed. Richard Kearney) (Guernsey, 1992, p. 103).

The Road to Emmaus[1]
(Luke 24: 13–35)

I wish to talk on 'the authority of the Church in a multicultural Europe', in connection with section 29 of the *Instrumentum Laboris*. I speak in my own name.

At the trial of those who plotted to kill Hitler, in July 1944, the judge said: 'We National Socialists and you Christians have only one thing in common: we both claim the whole person.' Christianity makes an absolute claim for Christ: He is the Alpha and the Omega. Yet in our society any absolute claim appears totalitarian and suspect.

Europe in the twentieth century has been crucified by ideologies which made absolute claims: communism, fascism, nazism. A multicultural society rejects such claims. People, including Christians, find meaning in a variety of sources: their family life, politics, national or ethnic identities, their football club, even their religion. Even many committed Catholics are suspicious of any absolute claim. For example, some Catholics will accept the Church's social teaching but resent any intrusion in their private life. Others will accept the authority of the Church over sexual behaviour, but be embarrassed when it criticizes capitalism. In a multicultural society we pick and choose from the supermarket shelves of values. So how can we make an absolute claim for Christ?

But the crisis of authority we experience within the Church is merely a symptom of a wider crisis of authority in our European culture since the Enlightenment. To grossly oversimplify, it is felt that any external authority which tells me what I should believe or do, is suspect. To submit to another's word would be to lose my freedom and autonomy. This is a suspicion which haunts even many

Christians in Europe. We cannot respond to that fear by just asserting the authority of the Church ever more strongly. People may either resist or take no notice. And as St Thomas Aquinas, a great authority, said, the appeal to authority is the weakest argument.

What then are we to do? I found as I prepared these words that it is easier to pose the question than to find the answer. But the story of the journey to Emmaus offers us a few clues, because it tells of how a crisis of authority is overcome.

The disciples flee from Jerusalem. They have heard the witness of the women, but they are not convinced. As so often, the men did not listen to the women! 'Some of us went to the tomb, and found it as the women said: but him they did not see.' The women proclaimed their faith but without effect. This is sometimes our experience in Europe. We proclaim our faith with all confidence, as we must, but our witness will often not have authority. 'Him, we did not see.'

Jesus begins by trying to make them understand: 'Beginning with Moses and all the prophets he interpreted to them in all the scriptures the things concerning himself.' Faced with their blindness, he explains the scriptures. He struggles with their minds. He tries to make sense of their experience. Here we see the *authority of reason*. It is a first step: 'Did not our hearts burn within us, as he talked to us on the road.' We in the Church must appeal to the minds of men and women, showing in the gospel the meaning of their experience. We must appeal to reason. But this will not be enough. For as the Encyclical *Fides et Ratio* has shown, our society is marked by a crisis of confidence in reason too. So there must be more.

Jesus walks with the disciples as they flee. To leave Jerusalem is, for Luke, an act of despair. Like many people in the Church today they are disappointed, disillusioned. Jesus does not stop them, or bar their way. He walks with them, accepts their hospitality and enters their house, eats their bread. This ends their journey away from faith.

To have convincing authority we must share the journeys of people, enter their fears, be touched by their disappointments, their questions, their failures and doubts. Often we speak about people: about women, about the poor and the immigrants, about the divorced, those who have abortions, about prisoners, people with AIDS, homosexuals, drug addicts. But our words for Christ will not have real authority unless we, in a sense, give authority to *their* experience, enter their homes, receive their hospitality, learn their language, eat their bread, accept from what they have to offer. This is dangerous. People will misunderstand and accuse us of being mixed up with the wrong people. But there is a good precedent for that.

Finally the disciples' eyes are opened when they see him in the breaking of bread. Our words will have authority if they are seen to welcome in the outsiders, to gather in people to the Kingdom. One of our Dominican brethren who lives in the war zone in Colombia acquired great authority on all sides of the conflict. He invited everyone to come to the parish every Saturday: the terrorists, the army, the paramilitaries, the people. They could eat and drink and play football, as long as they left their guns outside. He had authority because he gathered them together.

And the culmination of the story of Emmaus is that the disciples go back to Jerusalem to proclaim what they have seen. The crisis of authority is resolved not by their submission but in their proclamation. They become authorities themselves. It is a word that has authority *over* us, and also it gives authority *to* us.

Like the women we must indeed confidently proclaim our faith. But we cannot respond to the crisis of authority just by asserting our faith ever more strongly, hammering away. For many people this will confirm their fears about the nature of Church authority, that it is oppressive and destructive of their proper freedom. We show that the Word we proclaim does not just stand over and against us. It is more intimate to our being than any word we could speak; it made us and it enters the darkest places of the human heart, and offers us all a home. Then we will all be able to speak of the absolute claim of Christ with authority, and show it to offer us true freedom.

1   A speech given at the Second Synod of Bishops on Europe, October 1999.

Part Four

Living the Gospel

Does Doctrine Indoctrinate?

Note: Adapted from a talk originally given in 1991 to a conference of Primary and Secondary Headteachers in the Archdiocese of Wesminster.

A few months ago, while I was driving up the M1, I listened to a radio programme on inner London schools and their crises, with the drift to the private sector and the shortage of pupils and teachers. One of the people interviewed was a prep school headmaster who explained that parents must realize that they had an important product to market; it needed investment in the right equipment, the right packaging, but would eventually yield a handsome dividend. Eventually I realized that these particular commodities were eight-year-old children. Surely there is something blasphemous about the idea that a child might be thought of as a product. It was because he found English children for sale in the slave market that St Gregory the Great dispatched St Augustine to convert the English. He might well feel that the time was ripe for another evangelization.

This sort of perception is becoming common in the world of education, as schools increasingly come to be thought of as businesses which must run their own finances and be in competition with each other for the best pupils. Headteachers will be under pressure to employ less-experienced teachers so as to save on the salaries, and be tempted to dump their best teachers. But surely there is something deeply repellent about thinking of schools as businesses and children as commodities. Cardinal Hume said in his speech to the North of England Education Conference in Newcastle in 1990:

> 'I believe that the fostering of competition among schools and the introduction of commercial concepts is an undesirable and dangerous development ... Market forces have a part to play in society but they

determine, in the main, only transactions about goods and services that can be bought and sold. Some of the most important functions in society, some of the supremely human qualities of mind and heart carry no price-tag, cannot be quantified, are above the rough-and-ready requirements of supply and demand. But without them human community and relationships and growth are manifestly impossible.[1]

A Catholic community

What does it mean for a school to be a Catholic community? The first thing that we have to do as Catholics is to spot how there are ways of talking and thinking which, as the Cardinal said, threaten a school being any sort of community at all. There can be no human community if you think that what binds us together is the market.

It would be convenient to be able to blame Mrs Thatcher for this corruption, but that would be untruthful. This transformation of our language has been going on for at least 200 years. Karl Polanyi wrote a book called *The Great Transformation: The Political and Economic Origins of Our Time*, in which he argued that the last 200 years have seen the development of the 'commodity fiction', most specifically the illusion that land, labour and money were products to be placed on the market:

> Labour is only another name for a human activity which goes with life itself, which in its turn is not produced for sale but for entirely different reasons, nor can that activity be detached from the rest of life, be stored or mobilized; land is only another name for nature, which is not produced by man; actual money, finally, is merely a token of purchasing power which, as a rule, is not produced at all, but comes into being through the mechanism of banking or state finance. None of them is produced for sale. The commodity description of labour, land and money is entirely fictitious.[2]

It is a fiction that is deeply harmful to society:

> No society could stand the effects of such a system of crude fictions even for the shortest stretch of time unless its human and natural substance as well as its business organisation were protected against the ravages of this satanic mill.[3]

In recent years this dehumanizing illusion has become rampant. The Government has considered privatizing the prisons, hospitals are being made into profit-making concerns. It is said that a Tory think-tank has even considered privatizing the Church of England, which has excellent inner-city sales points – called churches – and 10,000 sales people, previously known as vicars, who can enter into vigorous competition to increase their share of the market.

Divine vocation

This is not a party-political but a deeply religious matter, because it is our vocation to talk of the world aright, to call things by their proper names. We are those beings whom God created to use language to celebrate the world that He has made.

C. S. Lewis argued with Helen Gardner about which human being they would most like to meet when they went to heaven. Lewis said, 'I have no difficulty in deciding. I want to meet Adam.' As he once wrote:

> He alone of all men [excuse the sexist language] 'had been in Eden, in the garden of God, he had walked up and down in the midst of the stones of fire.' He was endowed, says Athanasius, with a 'vision of God so far-reaching that he could contemplate the eternity of the Divine Essence and the coming operations of His Word.' He was 'a heavenly being' according to St Ambrose, who breathed the aether and was accustomed to converse with God face to face.[4]

Helen Gardner disagreed. She thought that if there was such a person he was probably a Neanderthal ape-like creature, whose conversation would be rather boring.

They were both right, but in different ways. The story of our first parents says something fundamental about what it means to be a human being. It tells of how we were called to be God's friends, to share his life. It was that intimacy with God that enabled Adam to know what to call the animals. Their names were not casual labels slapped on at random. Because of his friendship with the Creator he knew the creation, and indeed in giving the animals their names he was helping God bring an ordered, meaningful world into existence, overthrowing chaos. When we teach children how to speak about the world, to name the parts of a plant, to understand physics and chemistry or other cultures, we are initiating them into their divine vocation, to call things by their proper names, to be friends of the Creator. All true teaching is therefore a religious vocation which we practise as the children of Adam, the friend of God. When the serpent came Adam and Eve began to use language wrongly, to say that it was good to eat of the fruit that God had forbidden. This is what the racist does when he talks of black people as 'niggers' or the male chauvinist when he demeans women. The 'commodity fiction' is likewise a systematic misnaming of the world. When we can no longer see the creation as gift then the Giver disappears from sight.

Learning to see

In *Our Catholic Schools: Safeguarding and Developing their Catholic Identity*, it is written that headteachers are entrusted with ensuring that Catholicism permeates the whole of school life. Teachers are to disclose Christ 'with every gesture of their behaviour'. That may seem an impossible demand when the only gesture of Christ that comes to mind is the cleansing of the Temple or the cursing of the fig tree. What could it possibly mean? In what sense could religion be brought into everything that you do? Surely it must at least in part be in teaching children that it is their religious vocation to speak truthfully of all things, that all true learning brings one close to the Creator. Plato said that religion is the instinct for reality.

Seeing things just as they are may seem a straightforward task; the chemist just has to look down the microscope, the biologist must cut open the dead rat and see what is there, the historian check the dates etc. But one of the things that the ecological movement has taught us is that seeing things as they are is difficult; we have to learn not to look at things as merely usable, exploitable, in terms of their utility. There is a contemplative, disinterested perception that lets things be and delights in their existence. We have to learn this not only when looking at a rainforest but even at each other; it is where the pursuit of truth and the practice of prayer, study and morality, meet each other.

There is a story told about an old desert father of the fourth century who was walking along the road with his disciples and they saw a beautiful woman coming along on a donkey in the other direction. And the old man looked at her appreciatively while the disciples fixed their eyes on the ground lest they be led into temptation. A couple of miles later one of the disciples said: 'Father, why did you gaze at that lovely woman?' And the old man said, 'Oh, so you are still thinking about her, are you? You saw her only as a source of temptation. I saw her as one of the wonders of God's creation.' All education is helping people to see things as they are. And that is to say, it is ultimately learning to see things as created not a commodity but a gift.

If Adam's vocation was to call things by their proper names, then words matter. By speaking we can help bring about the world God desires, be co-creators with Him. We can speak words that create or destroy, words that edify, in the literal sense of 'build up', or suck out the life from people and degrade them. There is a creature that lives in ponds in America, called The Giant Water Bug. It creeps up on little frogs and sucks out their insides, leaving behind just a frog-shaped empty skin. We can speak to each other words that are like God's Word, bringing things to be, or in our speaking be like the Giant Water Bug, undoing God's world. Our words matter, and that is perhaps the most fundamental thing that we can teach our children.

In October 1990 Vaclav Havel was awarded a German peace prize. And the power of words, a power that he believes that we in the west have largely forgotten, was his theme. He wrote:

> You live in a country with considerable freedom of speech. All citizens without exception can avail themselves of that freedom for whatever purpose, and no one is obliged to pay the least attention, let alone worry their heads over it. You might therefore easily get the impression that I overrate the importance of words ... Yes, I really do inhabit a system in which words are capable of shaking the entire structure of government, where words can prove mightier than 10 military divisions, where Solzhenitsyn's words of truth were regarded as something so dangerous that it was necessary to bundle their author into an aeroplane and transport him. Yes, in the part of the world I inhabit the word Solidarity was capable of shaking an entire power bloc.[5]

Words matter

It is because words matter and have power that the sacraments are not magical moments in a mundane world. In these words of blessing and forgiveness, which transform bread into the Body of Christ, and set us free from sin, we see what all human language aspires to. Here we see the fulfilment of Adam's vocation, in which we share in the mystery of God's creative word. Emily Dickinson wrote:

Could mortal lip divine
The undeveloped freight
Of a delivered syllable,
    T'would crumble at the weight.[6]

This belief in the undelivered freight of the human word lies behind the whole Christian sacramental system. So when children are introduced to the sacraments, these are not included just to give a Catholic flavour to the course, but because they bring to light what it means to be the friends of God who help him bring about the New Creation. This is grace perfecting nature.

I have said a bit about why I think that all teaching is implicitly religious. But we are also asked to think about how a school can have a distinctly *Catholic* identity. In *Our Catholic Schools* we read that 'Every opportunity for Governors to take initiatives to give witness to the school's Catholic identity is important.'[7]

What does that mean? Does it mean having special celebrations, teaching the children about the saints, having pictures of the Pope on the wall? There is much to be said for these symbols of identity. Every community needs them if it is not going to disintegrate. But there is a curious tension built into the idea of being both 'distinctive' and 'Catholic', particular and universal. The more we assert the one, the less we seem to have of the other. And the temptation is either to fall back into a 'ghetto Catholicism', that defends the battlements and may be more about being Irish or Polish or Recusant than universal, or to fall into some wishy washy humanism that offers no more than a vague optimism, a belief that Jesus was a nice guy and that we must all do our own thing. I believe that it is a tension that is built into Christianity, which is the belief that this particular man, living in a particular time, brought life to all people. It is the tension that we try to hang on to when we say that the Church is both 'Roman' and 'Catholic'. If it was not Roman then it could not be a particular community, and if it was not Catholic, then it could not be a sign of the Kingdom.

Authority to teach

I believe that this tension in a school being 'distinctively Catholic' bubbles to the surface when we come to think about what it means to teach anything at all. The one thing that everyone knows about the Catholic Church is that it claims the authority to teach, and so do school teachers but usually in a rather different sense. Many teachers would believe that their vocation is to challenge, to put into question, to doubt the inherited tradition, to be undogmatic. So there is a deep problem about what it means to be 'a distinctively Catholic school', which revolves around what it means to teach. This is a problem that has been acute since the eighteenth-century Enlightenment, which saw itself as enlightened precisely because it put into question all that it had received; thinking meant doubting and the person who pursed truth began with scepticism. If that is how one thinks, and it is the underlying assumption of our whole intellectual culture, then the teaching Church stands for all that is narrow and obscurantist. To inherit a tradition is to be prejudiced. Dogma equals indoctrination.

I suspect that part of our problem in tracking down this 'distinctive identity of the Catholic School' is that we have largely bought this picture. Last year I was at a meeting for 600 Catholic sixth-formers and the principal of one sixth-form college told me that they did not teach their students any Catholic doctrine because at that age, 17 and 18, they were still too young. The presumption was that the teachings of the Church were opposed to teaching in the educational sense of the word. Dogmas close the mind and suffocate the intelligence and so can be no part of the school curriculum. To teach a child that God is three persons would be an assault on their intellect. There seems to be an in-built contradiction about the whole idea of a Catholic school. At best we are tempted by Harold Wilson's belief that theology is about counting the number of angels on a pinhead, at worst that it subverts all rigorous thought.

Another tradition

We are the heirs of another tradition, which maintains that believing and thinking are not mutually contradictory. As Anselm said, 'I believe in order to understand. For I believe even this: that I shall not understand unless I believe.'[8] The dogmas of the Church are not there to close our minds, to solve questions, to bring thinking to an end. What they are to do, in principle, is to open to us the dizzy, ineffable mysteries of God, which stretch our intellectual powers to and beyond their limits. That is why the Church founded all the ancient Universities of Europe, and saw them as cradles of faith. Dogma does not equal indoctrination, gullibility. On the contrary, as Chesterton once said, if you cease to believe in God the trouble is not that you will believe in nothing, but that you will believe anything. Hence the modern obsession with the occult, with Zodiac signs, witchcraft etc. Of course it is true that the Church has often been intolerant and hammered people over the head with doctrine instead of leading them into the mystery, but when this has happened we have not been true to our own central tradition.

Let me take just one example: Would you consider it appropriate to teach school children that Jesus is truly God and human? Leaving aside the question as to how one might communicate such a daunting mystery, would it be right and a proper part of education to actually teach this doctrine or would it be indoctrination, an assault on their dignity as rational beings whose minds must be opened? A Jesuit friend of mind told me that once he visited an RE class in Glasgow, and heard the children chanting

'The Father is not greater than the Son, the Son is not greater than the Spirit; they are all the same size; they are all the same size. The Father was not before the Son; the Son was not before the Spirit; they are all the same age; they are all the same age.'

This conjures up the terraces of Parkhead rather an initiation into a mystery.

There is one school of thought which would say that we must simply introduce children to a variety of possible beliefs and they must choose. They must discover what feels right to them, the belief with which they are most comfortable. That alone respects their freedom. This is a perfectly reasonable position but in the end, I suspect, it rests upon a definition of freedom that derives from the Market. One's freedom of belief is the freedom of the supermarket and so one would no more teach a child that Jesus is divine than one should teach him or her that Persil is the washing powder to buy. It looks like respect for the dignity of the child but it is not. What could be more patronizing than to tell someone: 'If you want to believe that God is a mushroom, then go ahead. If that is what you are comfortable with, then OK.'

The freedom to choose is an important right, and one which the Church has often failed to safeguard, but our tradition of doctrine has not evolved to limit choice but to expand the mind. Dogmas have not been defined to stop us buying rival brands of theological washing powder but to goad us into going on thinking, not settling for answers that are too small, too narrow. They are invitations to carry on exploration rather than to end all questioning. Let us consider the doctrine that Jesus is truly divine and human.

The mystery of God

In the fifth century this was the great debate of the day. When you went to buy bread, the baker tried to persuade you that the Father was greater than the Son; go to the public baths, and the attendant would argue in favour of the divinity of Christ. People argued passionately about theology then as we do about football now. If I may be forgiven a gross over-simplification, there were two rival camps. The Alexandrians had a beautiful theology of the divinity of Christ, for if God has not come to dwell with us, then how can we be saved? But it was sometimes hard to believe that their Christ was a real human being rather than a useful robot for the divinity. The Antiocheans, whose city had a more strongly democratic tradition, could only value a Christ who was fully human, who had known our struggles and suffered our pains and come to victory. But this human hero seemed to have a rather tenuous connection with the Second Person of the Trinity. So we find two theological traditions, each perfectly coherent, intellectually satisfying and corresponding to the political traditions of their adherents; for the Egyptians a God who came in splendour like a Pharoah, and for Antioch a hero of the city stadium. The sales-manager might say that each had the product tailored to their market.

At Chalcedon the whole Church gathered together and defined Jesus as truly God and truly human. This is the teaching that we have inherited. This was not an end of the exploration of the mystery of Christ. If anything it was the beginning. We were not offered a solution, a theology that tied up all the loose ends and meant that we could stop thinking. Rather the Church pushed Christians beyond two answers that were too small, too neat and tidy, into the glorious open spaces of the mystery of God. It eased Alexandrians and Antiocheans beyond pictures of Christ that too narrowly mirrored their own situations, a Christ who was merely 'relevant'. It is as if the Church were to insist to Oxford dons that Jesus is the one who turns the world upside down and brings freedom and liberation, and to Latin American theologians that the Christ is the eternal and unchanging Logos.

Thinking about the distinctive identity of the Catholic school may seem a luxury when schools and school teachers are struggling to survive at all. What I have tried to suggest that what our faith offers us is not just a bit extra to the curriculum, a few pictures on the wall and the occasional Mass. Our faith touches the most central concerns of any school, the power of words and the nature of teaching. Our children are neither commodities nor consumers, but the children of God, made to delight in the truth, and a truth that will set them free.

1   *Briefing*, 26 January 1990, p. 29.
2   p. 72.
3   *Ibid.* p. 73.
4   From *A Preface to Paradise Lost*, quoted in *C. S. Lewis: A Biography*, by A. N. Wilson (London, 1990, p. 210).
5   Speech in *The Independent*.
6   Emily Dickinson, 'A syllable'.
7   *Our Catholic Schools*, p. 11.
8   *Proslogion*, chapter 1.

Shrove Tuesday[1]

It is a great joy for me to be able to celebrate this very special day with you at Sant'Egidio.[2] Today is carnival time, *Mardi gras*, a day for laughter and celebration. Today is the day when, traditionally, the world was turned upside-down, when barriers between people were removed. People were happy: for a day, what divides us was ignored or overturned. Kings had to be servants and obey, while servants were kings. I suspect that, if the servants went a bit too far, the kings got their revenge the next day. Today, in some places, it's a day when men have to obey women and do the cooking, while women give the orders. Some people think that shouldn't be confined to carnival!

So carnival is not just an excuse for having a good time, for eating and drinking too much. It is a feast of hope, in which we celebrate our conviction that one day the world will be changed. Today we are separated from one another, by wealth, by nationality, by prejudices. But it won't always be like that, because God will make a new heaven and a new earth in which we shall all be one. That's a time to dream about!

The Bible is full of dreams. Isaiah dreams of a world in which the wolf will lie down with the lamb, a world filled with peace. Our society is tempted by fatalism; it's led to believe that nothing can ever truly change, that we can't do much about poverty or corruption. People call that realism. But as Christians we know that the only true realists are the dreamers.

I said that carnival invites us to dream, to dream of a transformed world. One of the reasons why I value the Sant-Egidio Community so much is precisely that it is the fruit of a group of young people who dared to dream. They dreamed that the divisions between rich and poor could disappear and that hearts could open. They had a dream and dared to make it reality. That's a good reason for coming here to celebrate carnival. This evening, I ask you to have dreams, impossible dreams, and to share them. There is a song that says if you dream alone your dreams will always be dreams, but that if two people dream the same thing they give birth to a new reality.

Some years ago, when I was young, I was in Trinidad at carnival time. In Trinidad, the great division between people is colour. The island's inhabitants descend from European, Indian, African and Chinese ancestors. What separates them most is colour: black, white, yellow. So, naturally, carnival is where these colour differences are abolished. Early in the morning, people are out in the streets dancing to steel bands, and carrying pots of paint which they throw at each other. I remember going back to the Dominican convent all the colours of the rainbow. I shall never forget the look on the friars' faces when we went into the refectory.

But it's not just a party: it's an invitation to dream of a world in which there are no separations based on colour or race. In the Kingdom of God, we shall all be brothers and sisters. In Europe, you can see growing intolerance towards strangers, towards those who are not like us. Everywhere in Europe you hear stories of growing violence against strangers, our brothers and sisters in Christ. This evening, let us dream that all this violence has come to an end and let us begin to set about making that happen. That might seem a mad dream, but with God nothing is impossible.

Rome is different from Trinidad. It's a very religious city – I am told – in which you are always very aware of the Church. Here, one of the major divisions was between those who were seen as good and those people judged to be bad, between saint and knave. But at carnival, then, people dreamed of doing away with all that. The tradition was to disguise oneself as either a cardinal or a prostitute. Suddenly, the streets were full of cardinals and prostitutes. It wasn't really an attack against the Church; it was proclaiming a dream, a dream in which the extremes, those who were farthest apart from each other, were united, bound by friendship. It symbolized the end of the boundaries between those on the inside and those on the outside of the community.

So let us dream too; let us dream of a world in which no one is excluded from the community. What can that mean, here in Rome? Perhaps people suffering from AIDS whom we should welcome as our friends. Let us dream of a world in which no-one is despised.

I have spoken of two dreams: that of breaking down barriers between us and strangers – and I'm a stranger too! – and that of breaking down barriers that make some people be judged as good and others as despicable. And then there are the personal dreams, of which it is difficult to speak clearly. Do we dare to dream that fabulous dream, that of setting aside everything that can distance us from God, the dream of holiness? Do we dare to dream of our personal transformation? Do we dare to dream of becoming loving persons?

Tomorrow, when the party's over, the time for penance will begin. Tomorrow, the Pope is coming to Santa Sabina to give the ashes. That in no way means giving up dreaming. It means that, to make your dreams move into reality, you have to be freed.

If we want to set out on the pilgrim way to the Kingdom of God, we need to travel light. Doing penance means freeing ourselves of anything that can weigh us down on the journey.

Next week, when I am due to leave for six weeks in Asia, from Pakistan to Japan, I shall go through the usual torments of packing my little blue bag. There are always the same problems. Do I really need four pairs or socks, or will three be enough? Do I need a change of trousers? Should I take my radio to listen to the BBC news? If I need to ask such questions setting off on a journey to Japan, just imagine what it would be like if I was setting off for the Kingdom of God!

As Jesus said in today's gospel, those who want to follow me must leave their family, their home, their land, their money. If we want to carry out our dreams of a new world, we have to strip ourselves of all unnecessary baggage. Dreamers should free themselves of their useless needs.

One of the greatest dreamers of our age was Martin Luther King, who had that great dream. He dreamed of the promised land, in which the children of slaves could sit down with the children of planters. It was a dangerous dream, and it cost him his life. If we want to dream of a new heaven and a new earth, and to work for it, that will be dangerous and may cost us our life also. Wherever I go in the world I see how far the members of religious orders who have great dreams – of a just world, of equality among human beings, of dialogue with Islam – are in danger of death.

During Lent we give up little things – cigarettes, sweets, drink. But that's just a way of training ourselves to have, if necessary, the courage to give up our lives.

The greatest of all dreamers was our Lord Jesus Christ. He dreamed of a world in which the poor would be happy and satisfied, the merciful receive mercy, those who suffer be consoled. It's true that that is a mad dream, the dream of heaven. But it was shown to be possible in his resurrection. In the resurrection, his dream became reality. Let us, during Lent, try to share his dream and to go with him towards Jerusalem, having a party on the way.

1   Sermon delivered to the community in February 1995.
2   Founded in Rome in 1968 on the initiative of Andrea Ricardi, the Sant'Egidio Community is a Lay Movement that now has 30,000 members. Its principal fields of action are service to the poor, ecumenism, interfaith dialogue and mediation in situations of civil war.

The Gift of Memory

Note: First published in *New Blackfriars*, November 1989 (pp. 531–7), and based on a talk given in London at a Pax Christi conference on 3 September 1989 marking the 50th anniversary of the outbreak of the Second World War.

We are told to remember the Second World War, but how? I was born just a few days after Hiroshima and Nagasaki. I have no stories to tell of my own. Maybe that does not matter. Remembering something as awful as the War can only happen later, long after it is over. To remember is not just to sit back and let the facts surface. It is the creative business of putting things together, re-membering, so that we discover for the first time what it was really like. Robert Kee was an RAF bomber who kept detailed diaries of the war, but afterwards they did not turn out to be of much help:

> For all the quite detailed evidence of these diary entries I can't add up a very coherent picture of how it really was to be in a bomber squadron in those days. There's nothing you could really get hold of if you were trying to write a proper historical account of it all ... No wonder it is those artists who recreate life rather than try to recapture it who, in one way, prove the good historians in the end.[1]

It is like the writing of the gospels. It took forty years before the disciples could tell the story of Jesus, and of how they betrayed him and ran away. It took about the same length of time that separates us from the Second World War before the disciples could cope with remembering what had happened, and so write the first gospel. Like them we are just getting to the point where we can begin to remember.

Primo Levi was an Italian Jew who was at Auschwitz for two

years. One day he was rebuked by another prisoner because he was not bothering to wash. Why wash? Because

> the Lager was a great machine to reduce us to beasts, we must not become beasts; that even in this place one can survive, to tell the story, to bear witness; and that to survive we must force ourselves to save at least the skeleton, the scaffolding, the form of civilisation.[2]

So one had to survive so that the memory would not perish. Levi emerged from Auschwitz as a man bursting to tell his story. As he writes in the opening poem of his book *If This is a Man,*

> I commend these words to you.
> Carve them in your hearts
> At home, in the street,
> Going to bed, rising;
> repeat them to your children.
> Or may your house fall apart,
> May Illness impede you,
> May your children turn their faces from you.

This echoes the *shema*, the daily Jewish prayer of remembrance of the commandments. To remember the Holocaust was the new commandment.

In the camp he had a dream, and it was a common dream, the dream that all the prisoners had. It is of no one listening to their story. They tell what happened, but everyone is indifferent. And indeed when Levi first published his book after the war, no one took much notice. When he wrote what I think was his last book, *The Drowned and the Saved*, before he committed suicide in 1987, he had come to see just how difficult it is to remember. The people who really touched bottom either did not survive or could not remember. The people who really knew the horror left no memories behind them. He wrote:

> We survivors are not the true witnesses ...; we are those who by their prevarications or abilities or good luck did not touch bottom. Those who did so, those who saw the Gorgon, have not returned to tell about it or have remained mute, but they are the 'Muslims' (*camp word for 'the helpless'*), the submerged, the complete witnesses, the ones whose deposition would have a general significance.[3]

The *Sonderkommandos* were the special squads of Jews who took people to the gas chambers, removed the bodies, extracted the gold teeth and the women's hair, sorted the shoes and after cremation took out the ashes. The Gestapo regularly eliminated these squads so that no one should survive to tell the story. And those that escaped have almost always been unable to talk.

For all the survivors there was the shame of gradually seeing what they had become, of letting the memories surface. There was the guilt of surviving when the best had died. It was then that so many of the survivors committed suicide. Their memories too are lost. So then it is not easy for us to remember what happened in the Holocaust. We must never forget, but the worst is impossible to remember.

If the Jews find it difficult to remember the Holocaust, what about the Germans? What story can they tell? In 1961 Primo Levi's book *If this is a Man* was published in German translation. In his introduction he said that he wanted the book to have some echo in Germany, so that he could understand them. 'I am alive and I would like to understand you in order to judge you' (p. 143). It is fascinating to read some of the letters that he got back from Germany but they do not offer a way to understanding. One woman wrote,

> In your preface you express the desire to understand us Germans. You must believe us when we tell you that we ourselves are incapable of conceiving of ourselves or of what we have done. We are guilty. (p. 150)

In his speech to the Bundestag on the fortieth anniversary of the end of the War, President von Weizsacher said:

> All of us, whether guilty or not, old or young, must accept the past. We are all affected by its consequences and liable for it ... Anyone who closes his eyes to the past is blind to the present. Whoever refuses to remember the inhumanity is prone to new risks of infection.[4]

But how? What story can the Germans tell? The usual way that we preserve important memories of the past is by giving them a place in the history of the nation. The nation-state is the subject of our memories. It is the story of the nation that holds a society together. It is the hero of our stories, whether in glorious victory or brave defeat. After the end of the Second World War the British decided that the cause of all the trouble was the story that the Germans told of their past. They had seen how effective German propaganda was and wanted to have a go themselves. We had beaten their armies and now we had to win their minds. What was needed was, in the words of the *British War Zone Review*, December 1945, 'to effect a radical and lasting change of heart in the hard-working, efficient, inflammable, ruthless and war-loving German people.'[5] We had to give them a new history, to 'stamp out the whole tradition on which the German nation had been built.'[6] We had to get back behind Bismarck, back behind German nationalism to the liberal traditions of early nineteenth-century Germany. Typically, we chose a public school headmaster, Robert Birley of Charterhouse, to be one of the people appointed to teach the Germans how to be British. He wrote to *The Times* on VE Day: 'Every means should be taken to persuade the Germans that they themselves had such a tradition, however completely forgotten ... Germany was a land of liberal thinkers.'

This still did not give the Germans a way of remembering the Holocaust. The only available model for remembering the past, the story of the nation-state, simply could not cope with that obscene event. What the War really showed was that that way of telling history was bankrupt. The ultimate consequence of that idolatry of the State was the Concentration Camp. So the story of the nation could not find a place for that memory. It is inconceivable. As the woman wrote, 'we are incapable of conceiving of ourselves or of what we have done.'

The temptation is either to forget that it happened, or to discover that someone else did it. The young blame the old, and the East Germans believe that it was nothing to do with them. A correspondent of *The Financial Times* wrote about celebrations for the fortieth anniversary of the end of the War:

> In nearly all accounts, the Nazis and their helpers are portrayed as a strangely alien people who were fought at every turn by upright German anti-fascists. At times it appears to the younger East Germans as if East Germany itself had fought beside their wartime allies to crush the Nazis.

The easiest thing to do is to let the whole thing sink into oblivion. In 1976 a German educationalist, Dieter Bossman, did a survey of 110 German schools. He looked at 3042 essays on 'What I have heard about Hitler'. He read that Hitler was an Italian, a Communist, he fought in the Thirty Years War, he was the first man on the Moon, he was a CDU deputy in the Bundestag, he attacked his opponents, the Nazis, and sent them to the gas chambers.

What the War showed is that that whole way of telling world history is bankrupt. It leads to Auschwitz. It is that way of telling history that the victors still glory in. In 1982 a Gallup survey showed that 80 per cent of Americans were proud to be American, whereas 80 per cent of Germans were ashamed of their nationality. The history of the nation is deeply important for America, which has been described as 'the world's first and most successful ideological nation'.[7] President Reagan vigorously promoted the use of national and patriotic history as a way of binding American society together and promoting the values of 'family, work, community and religion'.[8] We find it hard to realize that this is a history that blinds us to what we did in the War. We demand of the Germans that they remember their crimes, but we cannot see our own.

On 10 September General MacArthur issued the first 'civil liberties directive' which ordered the Japanese government to impose standards of truthfulness upon the press and radio. The Japanese papers did this, and started to criticize the American use of Atomic bombs. On 21 September a ten-point 'Press Code' was issued which forbade any criticism of the Allies. That is what truthfulness means for the victor.

Recently there have been proposals to open a Museum of German History in Bonn. Maybe it has already been opened. It must be created, said Chancellor Kohl, to teach the young 'where we Germans come from, who we are and where we stand.'[9] The CDU deputy, Alfred Dregger said, 'Without an elementary kind of patriotism which other nations take for granted, our nation will not be able to survive.' And Mrs Thatcher would completely agree. *The Observer* reported on 20 August that she has intervened to tell Kenneth Baker's successor, John MacGregor, that he must insist on there being more time devoted to British history. These patriotic, national tales are those that our modern nation-states need to survive. But the obscenity of the last War is one that explodes that way of telling history. Many Germans have seen that. We have not. We are the ones who suffer from the deeper amnesia. How then are we to remember?

We must turn for help to our Jewish cousins. They are a people constituted by remembrance, from the destruction of the first Temple and the exile through the desecration of the second Temple in the second century BC, the crushing of the rebellion against the Romans in the first century AD, the expulsion from Spain, the pogroms of Russia. Jewish life is saturated with the remembrance of suffering. During the medieval persecutions they would keep what they called *Memor books*, that recorded all that they had suffered. And they have not remembered as a nation-state. There was no national history between 70 AD and 1949. We, who are trying to learn what other tale can be told apart from that of the nation-state, can perhaps learn from them.

Elie Wiesel tells of two Jews who, in the midst of the terror in Germany, fleeing from the Gestapo, met in a cemetery. And they talk:

> 'What did you do . . . before?' 'I taught Jewish children to pray.' 'Really? Then heaven must have sent you to me. Teach me a prayer.' 'Which one?' 'The Kaddish' (that is the prayer of mourning for the dead) 'For whom?' 'For my children. For my mother. For my friends. For my illusions. For my lost years.' His friend made him recite Kaddish not once but ten times. It was not the Kaddish we know. We do not know, I fear we will never know, the Kaddish that two Jews recited in those days in an abandoned cemetery.[10]

The Jews had always remembered the endless sufferings of their people by turning them into prayer. Faced with every disaster they composed new prayers that somehow gave a place and meaning to what had happened. Prayer was that creative act by which they were able to remember. When these two Jews meet and pray in the abandoned cemetery, in the midst of the terror, they say a prayer, a *Kaddish*, that we do not know. Can we find that lost *Kaddish*? Can any prayer make sense of the Holocaust?

Albert Friedlander asks:

> Can there be prayers after the Holocaust? Theodor Adorno stated that no poetry could be written after Auschwitz. Prayer is poetry. Each catastrophe of Jewish life – the Destruction of the Temple, the blood-baths of the Crusades, the pogroms in Eastern Europe – was followed by an outpouring of Jewish prayers which fixed these events in the liturgy and in the memory of the Jewish people. The confessional prayers of the High Holy Days (*slichot*); the mourning chants of the Ninth of Av(*kinot*); the memorial prayers which included the martyrs of all the millenia of Jewish history: this was poetry of Jewish prayer for the times of darkness. Then came Auschwitz; and there were many scholars and rabbis who could no longer say the old prayers for the new event. The Holocaust was different. It was unique.' (*ibid.*, p. xix)

Is any prayer creative enough to redeem the event and make it bearable? For many Jews, there has been only silence and the extinction of faith. If prayer was the only way to remember, then the Second World War meant the end of prayer. If what happened could not be told in the framework of the story of the nation-state, for some it even broke apart the story of God's dealings with humanity. There is no story. So can there be any memory?

But Friedlander protests:

> We need words. We need altars and rituals and worship. We know that the enormity of our loss cannot be placed into human discourse; the *tremendum* of the *shoah* (the Holocaust) is somewhere beyond the boundary of human understanding. But there comes a time, as it came to Job after his long and brooding silence, when one has to stand up and cry out. That cry is prayer. It addresses God, and it addresses humanity. (*ibid.*, p. xx)

It must be possible to remember and so it must be possible to pray. Friedlander and Wiesel composed a beautiful series of meditations, to be used in liturgy in which they took up the stories of the War and placed them in prayer. They did this by placing them within the context of the story of Creation, the six days in which God made the world. That is the only story that could possibly bear those tales of destruction. But when they did this, something funny happened to the framework of the tale. The story of creation was disclosed as incomplete, filled with hints of lurking destruction. It was a story of how there was evening and there was morning and then there was evening. Chaos had not been entirely banished. The end of Creation is yet to come. No story just of the past is enough. 'Whatever response is evoked (to these prayers), let us remember that behind all our words is the reality of the time of destruction, and that, ahead of us, lies the time of creation' (p. 58).

This is above all what we learn from our Jewish brothers and sisters. No tale of the past is enough to bear the weight of this suffering for 'ahead of us lies the time of creation'. The only way to be able to remember the War is to tell a story that reaches out to a time of creation. The gospels teach us the same thing.

The most painful memory that the Church had to face was that it was the disciples themselves who had betrayed Christ, run away from him, denied him at the hour of his death. That was the suppressed memory and St John shows how remembrance comes as a gift, at the end, when the creative Spirit of God is given. The gospel is filled with hints that during the drama the disciples cannot see what is happening. During the cleansing of the Temple, when Jesus makes his triumphant entry into Jerusalem, they are blind. Afterwards they will remember and then they will see. When Jesus washes Peter's feet, on the night that Peter is to betray him, Peter is furious and says 'Lord, why do you wash my feet?' And Jesus answered 'What I am doing you do not know now, but afterwards you will understand.' (13:6)

Now is not the time of understanding. Now, during the crisis, during the betrayal, in the middle of the story, they cannot understand. Jesus says:

> These things I have spoken to you while I am still with you. But the Counsellor, the Holy Spirit, whom the Father will send in my name, he will teach you all things, and bring to your remembrance all that I have said to you. Peace I leave you. (14:25f)

The Spirit is the one who brings memory and peace.

At the end of the gospel, after the Resurrection, Jesus appears to the disciples and says 'Peace be with you' and he shows them his hands and his side. And he breathes the Holy Spirit upon them and says 'Whose sins you forgive they are forgiven; whose sins you retain they are retained.' It is now that they can see the wounds that they have caused. Now they can remember their betrayal and be forgiven. Now they know for the first time.

The breathing of the Spirit upon the disciples is a deliberate echo of the making of Adam at the very beginning. God takes the soil and forms Adam, and breathes his Spirit into him so that he becomes a living being. Now Jesus breathes the Spirit on the disciples, and makes them new human beings. The creation of humanity is something that is achieved at the end. It is then, in that time of re-creation, that they can dare to remember and to understand. That is the moment of truth and of forgiveness. Up to that moment they had no story to tell that could cope with something as obscene as their betrayal of their Lord. And the last chapter of John is of the healing of memory. Peter sits at a charcoal fire and three times Jesus asks him if he loves him, just as three times at a charcoal fire in the High Priest's palace Peter had denied knowing him. Now he heals that absence of memory, of the time when he forgot who Jesus was and who he himself was. 'Ahead of us lies the time of creation.'

The Baal Shem Tov, a great hasid, said, 'To forget is to prolong the exile and to remember is the beginning of redemption'. Remembrance is a sort of home-coming. It is the common memory that makes the home. And it is only at the end of the gospel, in the gift of memory, that the home, the Church, is formed. For to remember is to re-remember, to assemble the members, the limbs of the Body. In this moment of remembrance they come home to each other.

Can we remember the War as long as the subject of our stories is the Nation? It has been hard for the Germans to remember all that happened in the last War, because the sort of story which helps us to hold on to our identities is that of the nation-state. And that is a story that simply cannot make sense of this obscenity. We may demand of them that they remember but what story are they to tell? We too are still in the grip of just this story, of us in 'our finest hour'. And so we cannot remember what we did at Dresden, at Hiroshima and Nagasaki, every night in raid after raid, in the unimaginable brutality of war. We are like the disciples who could remember how it was the Romans and the Jews who killed Jesus, but it took them 40 years to remember that it was they themselves who killed him too. What we have to do is to remember for the first time what we all did in the War, what humanity did to itself. But to remember that we have to find ourselves one with others, not held in separation and otherness by nationalism. It is only a story that gathers us together, as God forms one humanity out of his children, a story that re-members us, that will let us recall what we have done.

After the War, the British went to Germany as teachers with a message. The Germans had 'to unlearn that it was the state which legitimated the individual rather than the other way round.'[11] The Germans had to be freed from idolizing of the State. The irony is that our own policies show that this is just what we now do. The policy of nuclear deterrence is an idolatry of the State. As Roger Ruston writes:

> But in so far as we are prepared to transgress *all* moral limits in the service of any person or collectivity, we treat them as a god. In a real sense, usually obscured from us by the modern separation of religion and politics, we have fallen into idolatry. We have made a god of the state.[12]

Our policy of possessing and threatening to use nuclear weapons means that the story we tell of ourselves is one that makes the State absolute and so God. It is a story that therefore ultimately holds us apart from each other and denies our common humanity. Primo Levi said that 'Many people – many nations – can find themselves holding, more or less wittingly, that "every stranger is an enemy" '.[13] And the logical conclusion of that is the Lager, Auschwitz, and the threat to annihilate whole populations of innocent people with nuclear weapons.

It is only an end to the idolatry of the State and the worship of the one true God who would make of us one humanity, that would let us see what we have done and been. Then we can tell a story that promises ahead the time of creation and of memory. Then we will know the Peace of Christ. Then we will remember and be re-membered, One Body.

1   P. Fussell, *The Great War and Modern Memory*, London, 1975, p. 311.
2   *If This is a Man*, London, 1969, p. 47.
3   *The Drowned and the Saved*, London, 1988, p. 63f.
4   Quoted by J. Ardagh, *Germany and the Germans*, London, 1987, p. 399f.
5   Quoted in N. Pronay and K. Wilson (eds), *The Political Re-Education of Germany and her Allies after World War II*, London and Sydney 1985, p. 88.
6   *Ibid.*, p. 27.
7   Pronay and Wilson, *op. cit.*, p. 11.
8   H. J. Key, 'History hi-jacked'. *Times Higher Education Supplement*, 6.2. 1987, p. 13.
9   *Times Higher Education Supplement*, 24 October 1986.
10 Elie Wiesel and Albert Friedlander, *The Six Days of Destruction, Meditations towards Hope*, Oxford 1988, p. 50.
11 Pronay and Wilson *op. cit.*, p. 1.
12 'The Idols of Security', in Alan Race (ed.), *Theology Against the Nuclear Horizon*, London 1988, p. 156.
13 *Op. cit.*, p. 15.

Time and Telling: How to Read Biblical Stories

Note: First published in *New Blackfriars*, March 1991, pp. 131–9.

There is probably no more serious threat to the Church throughout the world than the multiplication of fundamentalist sects. According to Robin Gill, 'Fundamentalism may be defined tentatively as a system of beliefs and practices which treat scriptural absolutism as the way to counter the pluralism and relativism engendered by modernity.'[1] In our new 'age of anxiety', they offer certainty and security. God has spoken and He has spoken clearly and this is what He has said. A proper analysis of fundamentalism would have to examine its rise in various forms in different faiths, including our own, and its political and social implications. In this article I wish to perform the much more limited task of suggesting how it is that a fundamentalist reading of the text relies upon thoroughly modern presuppositions as to how a text should be read. It is as contemporary as the relativism against which it protests. All narrative assumes a particular perception of space and time, the fundamental framework of any story. If we wish to break the hold of such a literalistic reading of the text we must become sensitive to its conventions of chronology and geography. Upon what clock and map does it rely? In particular I wish to suggest that a fundamentalist reading of scripture relies upon a modern understanding of time.[2] Let us start with St John's account of the death of Christ:

> Since it was the day of Preparation, in order to prevent the bodies from remaining on the cross on the sabbath (for that sabbath was a high day), the Jews asked Pilate that their legs might be broken, and that they might be taken away. So the soldiers came and broke the legs of the first, and of

the other who had been crucified with him; and when they came to Jesus and saw that he was already dead, they did not break his legs. But one of the soldiers pierced his side with a spear, and at once there came out blood and water. (19:31–4)

The Evangelist insists that this is a true account of what happened – 'This is vouched for by an eyewitness, whose evidence is to be trusted' (v. 35). But what does that entail? What sort of eye is in question? If an extraterrestrial being armed with a video recorder had shot a film sequence, would it have confirmed these details? For a fundamentalist, this would be so because the true eyewitness is the impartial eye, the disengaged observer without preconception, who stands on the edge of the crowd simply receptive to sense data, like the scientist gazing down his microscope. But this is only one way of being an eyewitness. Most Christians in the early centuries would also have believed that John gives us a true eyewitness account, but the eyewitness was never merely a passive recipient of sense impressions but a participant, who brought with him or her stories and traditions that moulded and structured a perception of the event. And this is evident in their understanding of time.

Jesus' side is opened and out flows water and blood, just as Adam's side was opened when Eve was created. And it was common in patristic exegesis to see here a reference to the New Adam bringing forth the New Eve, the Church with her sacraments of baptism and eucharist. This event is not just the death of a man in the third decade of the first century. It is also the time of creation, in which God's making of humanity comes to some sort of completion, just as is that eighth day after the Resurrection when Jesus will breathe the Holy Spirit on the disciples as God breathed his Spirit on the first Adam so that he became a living being. But yet another time is evoked too. John has advanced the time of Jesus' death, as given by the synoptic tradition, by twenty four hours so that now he dies at the time that the paschal lambs are slaughtered in the Temple; the Temple liturgy also laid down that their limbs are not to be broken. This is the time of the new Exodus from sin and death. So three times are evoked, of Creation, of the Exodus, of the slaughter of paschal lambs, to describe the death of this man on the hill.

Le Goff once wrote that

Perhaps the most important way the urban bourgeoisie spread its culture was the revolution it effected in the mental categories of medieval man. The most spectacular of these revolutions, without a doubt, was the one that concerned the concept and measurement of time.[3]

It has been said that since the Enlightenment we have lived in 'homogeneous, empty time', to use the phrase of Walter Benjamin.[4] It is the time of physics. It took the invention of the modern mechanical clock with its 'verge and foliot escapement' before we could perceive time in this way. There was an intimate link, though the patterns of causality are too complex to be unilinear, between a technological development and the eventual formulation of Newton's definition of time: 'Absolute, true and mathematical time, of itself and from its own nature, flows equably without relation to anything external.'[5]

One of the most famous early mechanical clocks was the astrarium of Giovanni de Dondi, designed in the mid-fourteenth century. Its main purpose was not so much to tell the time as to demonstrate the revolution of the stars and the planets. It was a mechanical representation of the universe, a miniature planetarium. Such mechanisms became extremely popular and are symptomatic of the transition from one perception of time to another. To discover what happened we must return to the Bible and see what sense was given to the earliest of all clocks, the revolution of the stars.

According to the first chapter of Genesis, 'God said "Let there be lights in the vault of the heavens to separate day from night, and let them serve as signs both for festivals and for seasons and years." (v. 14)' So the passage of the stars does not merely indicate the passage of time. They tell us when to celebrate the festivals, the moments for praising God. Their calendar marks the rhythm of the liturgy. Time is doxological. During Jesus' lifetime, at the end of each month the court of priests gathered to hear the first witnesses come and swear that the light of the new moon had been spotted. Then the chief of the court of priests would declare 'It is hallowed' and all the people answered 'It is hallowed; it is hallowed', and bonfires would be lit to proclaim the new month to the world.[6] The beginning of the month was a holy event. Time was diffused from the Temple.

Since the stars marked out the moments for praising God, it was only right and proper that they should join in too. God asks Job where he was when 'the morning stars sang together, and all the sons of God shouted for joy' (38:7). The sky was a vast choir of praise. No doubt the stars had originally been minor deities, demoted to musicians. So the revolving of the heavens was no impersonal mechanism that would carry on turning after God had given it an initial push, but the objective sign and sacrament of God's will and purpose, that his name would be praised.

It followed that it was of vital importance to possess the right and true calendar. There was no possibility of participating in the celestial liturgy if one was a day out. The Sabbath rest was a sharing in the rest of the of the heavenly court. Communities established their identities by their calendars. The Essences on the Dead Sea had a different liturgical *Ordo* from the Jerusalem Temple, as did the Book of Enoch. The wicked stars are those which fail to rise and set on time and so mislead the faithful (1 Enoch 18:12).

Raymond Brown has demonstrated that the first part of John's gospel shows how Jesus replaces the principal celebrations of the Jewish liturgy. He is the fulfilment of the Temple, the Sabbath, the Passover, the Feast of Tabernacles, and the Feast of Dedication. He is the new paschal lamb, and the source of living water. That is to say that the revolution of the stars and planets, the rising and setting of the sun and moon, the whole rhythm of the cosmos, finds its purpose in him. It is in him that the will of God becomes manifest and God's praise is made perfect.

If one's perception of time is shaped by the recurrence of the festivals and the revolutions of the stars, then the time structure of one's stories will be both repetitive and sequential. During the Babylonian Exile the Jews had to live within a culture that had both a sense of the passage of history and of liturgical cycle. Every year the New Year ceremonies in Esanglia, the Temple of Marduk, included the recitation on the fourth day of the *Enuma Elish* ('When on High'), the story of how Marduk slaughtered the sea monster Tiamat and created the world. Every year the original order of the universe was evoked and restored; every year was a new year and a return to the beginning of time. And when the Jews watched the gorgeous processions, the celebrations of a cosmic order that found expression in the power of Babylon, they must have wondered what story they themselves could tell and what time might promise. This is one of the stories that they came to share:

Awake, awake, put on strength,
O arm of the Lord;
   awake, as in days of old,
     the generations of long ago.
Was it not thou that didst cut Rahab in pieces,
that didst pierce the dragon?
Was it not thou that didst dry up the sea,
the waters of the great deep;
that didst make the depths of the sea a way
for the redeemed to pass over?
And the ransomed of the Lord shall return,
and come to Zion with singing;
everlasting joy shall be upon their heads;
they shall obtain joy and gladness,
and sorrow and sighing shall pass away.

(Isaiah 51:9–10)

This too is a story of the beginning, the slaughter of a primeval sea monster, only it is Rahab rather than Tiamat. But historical events are not in this case a return to an original order. Rather, the story of creation is used to describe the event of the Exodus and the passage through the Red Sea. And both these events have come to prefigure a future event, the return home from Babylon. So time is neither simply cyclical nor sequential, but spiralling through a history that encompasses repetition and difference. To tell the story aright is to detect the resonance, catch the echoes of this rich rhythm of time which is neither homogeneous nor empty.

If one's narratives are structured by this liturgical time, then clearly events which are linked in God's salvific purpose, moments of redemption or destruction, must have this relationship embedded in the calendar. They are, in some sense, the same event and so occupy the same liturgical locus. So, in the time of Jesus, it was believed that Abraham must have taken Isaac to be sacrificed on Mount Moriah on the fifteenth Nissan, the day of the Passover. The revolution of the stars, the messengers of God's will, binds together events which bear the same marks of God's purpose. The lamb that is slaughtered in the Temple is the lamb that was found in the bush and so to talk of each in terms of the other is to tell a truthful history.

One example of this 'liturgical synchronicity' is the Haggadah of the Passover, in which every victory over God's enemies has been carefully timed to occur on this same night of liberation:

Thou, O Lord, didst destroy the head of each firstborn on the night of
the celebration of Pesach; But thy firstborn, O Almighty, didst Thou
pass over because of the blood of the sacrifice of Pesach,
With which my doors were marked, so that the destroyer should not
enter on Pesach;
The enclosed city (Jericho) fell on Pesach;
Midian was destroyed by means of the barley cake of the Omer on
Pesach;
The princes of Pul and Lud were consumed at the very moment when
the sacrifice smoked on Pesach.
He (The King) stayed yet one more day in Nob until the advent of the
time of Pesach;
An invisible hand wrote prophesying the destruction of Zul (Babylon)
on Pesach. Just when the royal table was magnificently decked on
Pesach. . . .
The moment will one day come at which Thou wilt bring that double
misfortune on Utsis (Edom) on Pesach.
Thy hand will then be victorious, thy right hand exalted, as on that night
whereon Thou didst institute the festival of Pesach.[7]

History was not, as Henry Ford said, just 'one damn thing after
another'. To tell it truthfully one must detect the echoes and
ramifications of events which began long before. When Jesus is
tempted in the wilderness, then Israel at last makes its way through
the desert to the Promised land without sinning; when Jesus goes to
his Passion carrying his cross, then here is Isaac on his way to Mount
Moriah; when Jesus' side is opened on the cross and out pours blood
and water, then the creation of Adam and Eve comes to completion.
The true eyewitness is the one who participates in the events of
redemption rather than the mythical, impassive and uninvolved
bystander. Those who can really see what is happening are the
ransomed who 'come to Zion with singing'. The Babylonian melon
seller who might have stood by the roadside watching a band of
ragged refugees going home could not have told the true story. He
did not have the right calendar. He did not understand the meaning
of the rising and setting of the stars and planets.

There could no more be homogeneous and empty space than
homogeneous and empty time. A neutral geography was as
unimaginable as a history told from no one's point of view. A
map of the world is a picture of God's will and at its centre is
Jerusalem, the world's navel, and at the centre of Jerusalem the holy
mountain, with the Temple, a microcosm of the Universe. So the

Temple was a picture of space, as the calendar was a picture of time. Events which had the same meaning must have occurred in the same place.

The mountain of Isaac's sacrifice must be the same as the mountain upon which the lambs are now sacrificed. This was where Adam was created from the dust of the Temple site, and it was on this mountain that Adam lived after he was expelled from Eden awaiting the redemption that would be offered on this same mountain. It was here that Noah built an altar to offer sacrifice after the Flood. Logically one might have hoped that God would have offered the tablets of the Law to the Israelites here rather a few hundred miles south on Mt Sinai. But the Jews were not deterred: 'Whence did Sinai come? R. Jose taught: Out of Mount Moriah; out of the place where our father Isaac had been bound as a sacrifice, Sinai plucked itself out as a priest's portion is plucked out of the bread.'[8]

There are two ways to loosen the hold of a particular way of seeing the world and so become attuned to other narrative conventions. One is to describe how other people see time and space, and this I have done briefly. Another way is to recount the genesis of our own way of describing events. This I shall do even more sketchily.

From classical times until the end of the Middle Ages water clocks were widely used. They were not very accurate and immensely complicated. In part this was due to the fact that the hours that they measured varied according to the time of the year. An hour was a twelfth part of the day or night time and so was constantly lengthening or diminishing. With the mechanical clock we have the appearance of a standard and unvarying hour of sixty minutes. Time no longer reflected the rising and setting of the sun. It was no longer liturgical time, and the hours were no longer the hours of the Office, of the praise of God. Instead of the *très riches heures* of the Duc de Berry one has the standard hour which determined work in the textile industry of northern Italy. Instead of holy time, the calendar of holy days and festivals, of fasting and feasting, time became secular. The Puritan calendar was symptomatic of the emergence of a new perception of time. With the invention of the watch, time became private rather than necessarily communal. It is interesting that one of the first watches we know of in England was that given by Henry VIII to his fifth wife, Catherine Howard.

Let me quote Whitrow:

> The invention of an accurate mechanical clock had a tremendous influence on the concept of time itself. For, unlike the clocks that preceded it, which tended to be irregular in their operation, the improved mechanical clock when properly regulated could tick uniformly and continually for years on end, and so must have greatly strengthened belief in the homogeneity and continuity of time. The mechanical clock was therefore not only the prototype instrument for the mechanical conception of the universe but for the modern idea of time. An even more far-reaching influence has been claimed for it by Lewis Mumford, who has pointed out that 'It dissociated time from human events and helped create belief in an independent world of mathematically measurable sequences: the special world of science.'[9]

The stars went on turning, the sun rising and setting, but our sense of what it meant to live in a revolving cosmos was changed. It was no longer the embodiment of God's objective purpose, the shape of his saving will, but a mechanism that carried on ticking away like a great clock.

This meant that the way in which we told and heard narratives had to change; new stories for a new world. To describe the transformation of narrative conventions would be an immensely long and complex task and so I can do no more than refer to the work of Ian Watt, *The Rise of the Novel*, in which he shows how new scientific perception of reality, the world of Locke and Newton, was related to the appearance of stories told about ordinary people, with ordinary names, who gain their individual identity by being located in our time and space. The novels of Defoe and Fielding and Richardson have particular philosophical presuppositions which might not have been possible if it had not been for the evolution of the 'verge and foliot escapement' of the mechanical clock. Says Watt:

> The 'principle of individuation' accepted by Locke was that of existence at a particular locus in space and time; since, as he wrote, 'ideas become general by separating from the circumstances of time and space, so they become particular only when both these circumstances are specified'. In the same way the characters of the novel can only be individualised if they are set in a particularized time and place.[10]

When we ask whether we must believe that a scriptural text is true, literally true, then often we mean: 'But what would I have seen if I had been passing by at the time? What would the unprejudiced eye have spotted? If I had been at the feeding of the five thousand, would I have seen bits of bread and fish springing spontaneously into existence? Or would I have seen people embarrassedly producing rolls which they had kept tucked up their sleeves just in case ...?' When we ask such questions then I believe that we must answer that often we cannot know. We are asking questions which often imply a point of perception which the biblical authors could not have imagined. This is not to say, as I have argued elsewhere, that we can have no knowledge of historical events which underlie the biblical claims.[11] Rather, our eyewitnesses could not have imagined that the stance of disengagement gives one any privileged access to what 'really' is happening. Such a belief depends upon the assumption that a particular scientific culture offers the proper paradigm of all true knowledge, that the one who sees most truly is the scientist looking down his microscope or up his telescope.

It is, of course, an illusion to imagine that such a perspective upon the world is free of prejudice or preconception. It is deeply related, as Jurgen Habermas has shown in *Knowledge and Human Interests*, to a particular economic and political system. The 'disengaged ego' remains firmly in control of his environment. As Charles Taylor has written:

> The subject of disengagement and rational control has become a familiar modern figure. One might almost say it has become one way of construing ourselves, which we find it hard to shake off. It is one aspect of our inescapable contemporary sense of inwardness. As it develops to its full form through Locke and the Enlightenment thinkers he influenced, it becomes what I want to call the 'punctual self'. The key to this figure is that it gains control through disengagement.[12]

It is a disengagement that seeks ultimately to disincarnate us and that requires, as Nagel argues, 'a departure from a specifically human or even mammalian viewpoint'.[13] This is remote from a Christian belief in one who 'became flesh and dwelt among us, full of grace and truth'.

It is no accident that the stories that we tell, and the framework of space and time that they presuppose, are related to the emergence of industrial society. As Mumford wrote, 'the clock, not the steam engine, is the key to the modern industrial age.'[14] If the standard hour emerged because of the needs of the textile trade, so a standard national time, Greenwich Mean Time, emerged because of the need for a single time for the railway timetables. Indeed, it was first known as 'railway time'. Germany imposed a single national time in 1891 so as to enable military co-ordination in time of war. In fact, it was the need for simultaneous attack from the trenches in the First World War that finally made the wrist watch a normal item of male dress. So perceptions of space and time are never innocent. The disengagement is more apparent than real, for it is in view of a mastery of the environment. It is an epistemological stance which D. H. Lawrence effectively unmasks when he ponders on a visit to Bertrand Russell in Cambridge:

> What does Russell really want? He wants to keep his own established ego, his finite and ready-defined self intact, free from contact and connection. He wants to be ultimately a free agent. That is what they all want, ultimately ... so that in their own souls they can be independent little gods, referred to nowhere and to nothing, little mortal Absolutes, secure from questions.[15]

The study of Scripture can be demanding. Our ears are not attuned to the echoes and resonances, the barely suggested references, the hinted connections. Is it really necessary that one should need a degree to study the Word of God? Could the work of these simple fishermen be so complex and sophisticated? Did we have to wait all this time before the Word was unveiled to God's people? Perhaps it is hard work not because the narratives of the Bible are complex but because we are. We have evolved a particular perception of 'homogeneous and empty time' to which, anyway, neither novelists like Joyce nor scientists struggling with special theories of relativity grant unqualified assent anymore.

Study of Scripture invites us not only to enter a different narrative tradition but offers a deep critique of our way of looking at the world. It invites us to surrender the safe security of the disengaged reader, to lose our mastery, to give up being 'little mortal Absolutes', to entrust ourselves to the flow and thrust of a story beyond our control, like the one who, we believe, gave himself into other people's hands so that we might live.

1 *Competing Convictions*, London 1989, p. 23.
2 Unfortunately at the time of writing I had not had the benefit of

reading the interesting article by Albert Paretsky OP, 'Proleptic Recapitulation: Passover, Eucharist and God's saving acts', in *New Blackfriars*, December 1990, pp. 541–7.

3   *The Fontana Economic History of Europe: the Middle Ages*, quoted by G. J. Whitrow, in *Time in History: View of Time from Prehistory to the Present Day*, Oxford 1989, p. xi.

4   *Illuminations*, New York 1969, p. 261, quoted by Charles Taylor in *Sources of the Self: The Making of the Modern Identity*, Cambridge 1989, p. 288.

5   Quoted by Whitrow, *op. cit.*, p. 128.

6   S. Safrai and M. Stern (eds), *The Jewish People in the First Century*, Vol. 2, Assen 1976, p. 847.

7   Rabbi Dr Marcus Lehmann of Mainz, *The Passover Haggadah*, Jerusalem 1977, p. 320.

8   Terence L. Donaldson, *Jesus on the Mountain: A Study in Matthean Theology*, Sheffield 1985, pp. 55–7.

9   *Op. cit.* p. 127.

10 *The Rise of the Novel*, London 1957, p. 21.

11 *New Blackfriars*, March 1988.

12 *Op. cit.* p. 160.

13 *Mortal Questions*, Cambridge 1979, ch. 14.

14 *Loc. cit.*

15 *Collected Letters*, Vol. 1, p. 360, quoted by F. Kerr OP, *Theology After Wittgenstein*, Oxford, 1986, p. 60.

'Glorify God in your Bodies': 1 Corinthians 6: 12–20 as a Sexual Ethic

Note: First published in *New Blackfriars*, July/August 1986, pp. 306–14.

' "All things are lawful for me," but not all things are helpful' (v. 12). The Corinthians have a sexual ethic which starts from the question, 'What is allowed? What may I do?'. And doubtless they could quote Paul back to himself to show that since they were free from the law, they could do anything; 'For freedom Christ has set us free; stand fast therefore, and do not submit again to a yoke of slavery' (Galatians 5:1). It follows, then, that there can be no restrictions upon what is permitted to the Christian. We are allowed to perform any sexual acts that we wish.

Paul's reaction is not to revise his view that we are not under the Law but to suggest that asking what is permissible is not the right starting point. A proper sexual ethics is not, in the first place, about what is lawful, but about what is 'helpful'. In this passage Paul subverts the Corinthians' basic presuppositions in thinking about sexual ethics. Two thousand years later most Catholics need to submit to the same gentle subversion. The Church's teaching on sexuality is normally seen in terms of what is allowed or forbidden; sexual ethics are classified as 'permissive' or 'restrictive', and the Church authorities are usually happy to oblige by stating the limits of acceptable behaviour. We all need to submit to the Pauline therapy, and this works, like any decent therapy, by means of a dialogue between the patient and the therapist. All New Testament scholars agree that much of 1. Cor. 6:12–20 is Paul quoting from the Corinthians, but unfortunately they cannot agree where to put the quotation marks![1] This seems to be a plausible reconstruction of the therapeutic dialogue.

The Corinthians

All things are lawful to me

Paul

But not all things are helpful

All things are lawful for me

But I will not be enslaved by anything.

Food is meant for the stomach and the stomach for food and God will destroy both one and the other.

The body is not meant for immorality, but for the Lord, and the Lord for the body. And God raised the Lord and will also raise us up by his power. Do you not know that your bodies are members of Christ? Shall I therefore take the members of Christ and make them members of a prostitute? Never. Do you know that he who joins himself to a prostitute becomes one body with her? For, as it is written, 'The two shall become one flesh'. But he who is united with the Lord becomes one spirit with him. Shun immorality.

Every sin[2] which a man commits is outside the body.

The immoral man sins against his own body. Do you not know that your body is a temple of the Holy Spirit within you, which you have from God? You are not your own; you were bought with

> a price. So glorify God in your
> body.

The dialogue then moves off in a much less fashionable direction, which we will not bother to follow. Some people at Corinth have clearly decided that it is therefore much better to avoid sex altogether.

> Now concerning the matters
> about which you wrote, 'It is
> well for a man not to touch a
> woman',

> > but because of the temptation to
> > immorality each man should have
> > his own wife and each woman
> > her own husband etc.

It may seem curious to have extreme promiscuity and asceticism, everything and nothing being permitted, coexisting in the same community, but it is a common conjunction. Irenaeus tells us that we can find the same polarization within gnosticism a century later among the spiritual descendants of these Corinthians. Both extremes derive from the same despising of the body. If the body is unimportant one can either deduce that everything is permitted or nothing allowed. But Paul's starting point for a sexual ethic is different. We must ask what is 'helpful'.

'Helpfulness' seems to offer us a merely utilitarian criterion, but the English translation disguises the rich resonances of the Greek verb, *sumphero*. It means literally 'to bring together', as when, in Acts 19:19, the magicians bring their books together to burn them. What is 'helpful' is what knits the body of Christ together into unity, what brings us together in Christ. And it is no coincidence that Paul's sexual ethic starts with what 'brings together' since for him it is our bodiliness that enables us to be together. It is as bodily that we can be with each other. So the opening move away from the question of what is permissible to what brings together (*sumpherei*) is simply a consequence of his understanding of human sexuality.

Herbert McCabe wrote in a recent article,

> The ordinary way in which you are conscious of being bodily, conscious

of 'having a body', is being conscious of it as your way of being present to the world. Your body is first of all a means of communication and indeed it is the source of all others forms of communication.[3]

McCabe was not in fact talking about what Paul meant by the human body, but his remarks give an insight into the common purpose which unites the bewildering variety of ways in which Paul uses the word 'body'. It is the possibility of mutual presence, and a proper sexual ethic is one which respects that potentiality. J. Christiaan Beker isolates three distinct ways in which Paul believes we can be 'bodily'.[4] In the 'era of sin', before the coming of Christ, we had 'the body of sin', we lived in 'the flesh'. But when Paul talks about 'the sinful flesh' he is not suggesting that there is anything inherently sinful about being bodily. He is just suggesting that our unredeemed ways of living, of being bodily, went with a rejection of the other, the refusal of mutual presence. In that sense to live 'in the flesh' is to fail to be bodily in the proper sense of the word. It is 'unhelpful'; it does not 'bring together'. So he writes to the Galatians: 'Now the works of the flesh are plain: fornication, impurity, licentiousness, idolatry, sorcery, enmity, strife, jealousy, anger, selfishness, dissension, party spirit, envy, drunkenness, carousing, and the like' (5:19).

Another sense in which Paul can talk of our 'bodiliness' is when he holds out the hope for a risen body, 'the body of glory', 'the spiritual body'. In Chapter 15 we discover that the Corinthians seem to have found it unnecessary to believe in the resurrection of the body. It would have seemed to them to be a contradiction in terms. Salvation was salvation – release – from the body. But Paul, on the contrary, sees the resurrection as the raising of the body in glory and power (15:43); it is the flourishing of the body, the realization of its potentiality for presence. Our present condition, the context for a sexual ethic, is described by Paul as living in 'the mortal body' (*soma thneton*). It is the state of being in which we can choose whether to open ourselves up or close ourselves in. Beker says,

> The 'mortal body' expresses our historical existence 'between the times'; we are no longer the 'body of sin' and we do not have yet the 'spiritual body'. The multivalent contextual meaning of the term 'mortal body' yields a rich meaning: the Spirit indeed operates in the mortal body, so that we can glorify and worship God in our 'bodies' (1 Cor. 6:20; Rom. 12:1), whereas at the same time the body is subject to death, decay,

weakness and can even become synonymous with 'the flesh' (2 Cor. 4:11).[5]

So our present way of being bodily is essentially ambivalent. We can be bodily in a way that is open, spiritual, that prefigures the glorious body of the resurrection. Or we can slip back into being bodily in fleshly ways, egocentric, closed in, devouring one another. And we find the way to life not by asking what is lawful, permissible, but by asking what '*sumpherei*', what 'brings together', knits into unity.

The fundamental mistake that underlies the Corinthian position is shown by the next interchange in the therapy. The Corinthians say: 'Food is meant for the stomach and the stomach for food and God will destroy both the one and the other'. Paul's reply reflects the structure but subverts the presuppositions of the Corinthian statement: 'The body is not meant for immorality, but for the Lord, and the Lord for the body. And God raised the Lord, and will also raise us up by his power'. Murphy O'Connor has argued that the Corinthian slogan is supposed to show just how absurd is the whole idea of the resurrection of the body. The body cannot be the sphere of important moral decisions; it is essentially ethically irrelevant, since the whole thing will rot in the grave, eyes, heart, stomach and all. One's whole bodiliness belongs to an order that is passing away.

Paul opposes this, but not by standing up for the spiritual stature of the stomach. He would agree that the food and the stomach are going to be destroyed. He never argues for a resurrected stomach or a glorious kidney or a spiritual liver. In itself what we eat and drink is without importance, except in so far as it upsets or scandalizes our brethren. A couple of chapters later he says, 'Food will not commend us to God. We are not better off if we do not eat, and no better off if we do. Only take care lest this liberty of yours somehow become a stumbling block to the weak' (8:8f). So what you eat cannot be in itself of importance, except in so far as one might neglect the charity owed to one's brother or sister. Thus far Paul would broadly agree with the Corinthians. The mistake that they make is in thinking of the body as just a collection of organs, so that to believe in the resurrection of the body is to commit yourself to the resurrection of a whole collection of bits and pieces. But we have argued that this is not how Paul understood our bodiliness. It is a mode of presence. It may be true that in this 'mortal body' we can only be present to each other if we are in the happy possession of a stomach, but it is not the possession of a stomach as such that makes us bodily. And it is as those who are able to be present to each other that we are open to the life of the Spirit and await the resurrection. So over and against the Corinthian co-ordinates of food/stomach/ destruction, Paul gives us body/Lord/resurrection. Herbert McCabe has pointed out that the Corinthians have identified the ways in which the words 'stomach' and 'body' operate.[6] But stomach is a word that operates only univocally, on one level. When we apply it to things that are not bulges in the middle of our bodies, then we can only do so metaphorically, as when the Latins talked about Rome as the 'stomach' of the Empire. But 'body' is a word that one can use analogically; it operates on many different levels of meaning, from the 'body of sin' to the 'glorious body'. So it is not just a metaphor to talk of ourselves as being the 'body of Christ': 'Do you know that your bodies are members of Christ?'

So far Paul has been trying to sharpen our sense of what it might mean to be bodily, the proper context for any ethics. He now goes on to draw the consequences for a sexual morality:

> Shall I therefore take the members of Christ and make them members of a prostitute? Never. Do you not know that he who joins himself to a prostitute becomes one body with her? For, as it is written, 'The two shall become one flesh'. But he who is united to the Lord becomes one spirit with him. Shun immorality.

It is not clear why these Christian Corinthians had such an enthusiasm for sleeping with prostitutes. They may have been libertarians who celebrated their Christian freedom by visiting the brothels, or ascetics who satisfied their lusts while preserving the purity of their wives. In any case, they seem to have believed that to sleep with a prostitute was not in itself a particularly significant act. That is the meaning of their slogan, which is mistranslated in the RSV, 'Every sin which a man commits is outside the body'. In other words, sin cannot be a matter of what one does with one's body, but one'd mind. Murphy O'Connor expresses it thus: 'The physical body is morally irrelevant for sin takes place on an entirely different level of one's being. In the words of R. M. Grant "Motives, not actions, are important".'[7] And Paul's reply gives us the heart of his sexual ethic. 'The immoral man sins against his own body'. To be bodily is to be capable of giving yourself to someone; it is the possibility of mutual presence. To sleep with someone is to realize that possibility; it is to make a gift of oneself. And this is true regardless of one's motives or intentions. To sleep with a prostitute is to become truly one with her, one flesh. 'Do you not know that he who joins himself to a prostitute becomes one body with her? For, as it is written, "The two shall become one flesh".' So, for Paul, to sleep with a prostitute is to sin against one's own body because it is a negation of our bodiliness as the means of communication. It is an untruthful act; we become one with someone with whom we have no intention of sharing our lives. So what is at issue is not what is permissible or forbidden, but what the act means in and of itself. Paul's sexual ethic starts from the belief that, whatever one may intend or think or feel, one does in fact make a radical self-gift, become one body, when one sleeps with someone. A proper sexual ethic is one that helps one to live by the truth of what one does with one's body.

1 Corinthians is an exploration of what it means for us to live together in the body of Christ, the church, and so it is not surprising that Paul frequently refers to two of the most important bodily expressions of unity, food and sex. And these two threads intertwine significantly at the centre of the letter, Paul's discussion of the eucharist, the common meal which is the gift of a body. But the mistake that the Corinthians seem to have made was to identify the ways in which food and sex expressed and realized our bodiliness. Paul would largely, it seems, have agreed with them when they said that 'food is meant for the stomach and the stomach for food and God will destroy both the one and the other'. What you ate and drank was not *in itself* important, except in so far as it built up or destroyed the community. But sex is not a matter of the sexual organs in just the same way as food is a matter for the stomach. One could not say that 'sex is for the genitals and the genitals for sex, and God will destroy both the one and the other'. Sleeping with someone does not just symbolize or express a unity. It *is* being one with them. If being bodily is being present to someone, then one's sexuality is the realization of one's bodiliness in a way that eating is not. If one sits in a Wimpy bar and eats a hamburger in silence beside a stranger, this may be depressing. To casually and silently eat with a stranger may be a failure to express and explore one's common humanity, a lost opportunity, but it is hardly a sin! But it is quite different to casually and silently sleep with a stranger. That is not a failure to use a chance to be one with someone else; it is a lie,

for they would be one in a way that is denied for the rest of their lives. Now, sharing the eucharist is, of course, an activity that combines characteristics of eating with people and sleeping with them. Paul attacks the Corinthians for eating and drinking together in a way that expresses disunity and division. But this is not just a regrettable failure of charity, but a lie, since, as with sex, they are sharing a body: 'Whoever, therefore, eats the bread or drinks the cup of the Lord in an unworthy manner will be guilty of profaning the body and blood of the Lord' (11:27).

Paul's deep understanding of the significance of human sexuality is shown by how, in the last paragraph of this piece of the dialogue, he appeals to sexual imagery to describe our relationship with Christ:

> Do you not know that your body is a temple of the Holy Spirit within you, which you have from God? You are not your own; you were bought with a price. So glorify God in your body.

The 'body' that is the temple of the Holy Spirit is normally taken to be the individual body of each Corinthian – each of your bodies are temples of the Holy Spirit. That is a possible interpretation of the Greek if the single 'body' is taken in a distributive sense. But this is unlikely, and for two reasons. First of all, when Paul wishes to talk about their individual bodies in verse 15 he uses the plural form and so it would be curious if he shifted to the singular to mean the same thing four verses later. Secondly, the early church fathers found the Greek of this verse puzzling and when they quote it often change it to the plural. So it seems most plausible to argue that the body that is the temple of the Holy Spirit is the single Body of Christ. The proper context for understanding what it means for us to be sexual, bodily creatures is our membership of the Body of Christ. How we belong to each other sexually has to be discerned in the light of how we are one body in Christ. For the 'body of Christ' is not just a metaphor, as would be the case if it were a word that Paul used univocally, but the fruition of all that it means for us to be bodily and thus sexual. And so he describes our unity with Christ in sexual terms. How can we buy and own a prostitute, when we have been bought by Christ? We are his prostitutes, bought with a price.

The Pauline therapy has gradually shifted one's sense of what it means to be sexual, from sex as merely a bodily function to being the possibility of presence and union with another, and from the context of sexuality as being merely one's individual relationship with another to that of our belonging in the Body of Christ. It is a therapy which aims to heal one, to liberate one from fantasy and illusion. The nearest parallel that I can think of in the Bible is the eighth-century prophet Hosea's reaction to the fertility rites of his contemporaries. The Israelites had been seduced by the Canaanite fertility cult, which centred on the myth of Ba'al's marriage to his sister. This sexual mythology was copied, reenacted in the rites of the cult which brought fertility to the land. For a strict monotheist like Hosea, this sexual mythology was abominable. But rather than simply rejecting the whole language of sexuality as an appropriate way of talking about our relationship with God, he does something far more subtle. If you would be married to your God, then be truly married, not just in the repetition of a myth but in history. Instead of just ritually acting out the loss of fertility, the barrenness of winter, you will live it historically in exile. And when your God comes to restore you and marry you, it will not be just in the annual cult of springtime: 'And I will betroth you to me for ever; I will betroth you to me in righteousness and justice, in steadfast love and mercy. I will betroth you to me in faithfulness; and you shall know the Lord' (2:19f). He redeems the language of the fertility cult by moving beyond the fantasy of sexual mythology to marriage as a real and historical engagement.

The Pauline touchstone of a proper Christian sexual ethics would be whether it heals one of fantasy and helps one to live out historically the truth of one's sexuality. For the typical Western fear of the body still afflicts our society. The apparent obsession with sex is in fact a flight from sexuality in the deepest sense, the gift of oneself to another. It is a fear of engagement that afflicts the *voyeur*, as Susan Griffin has shown so well in her book *Pornography and Silence*: 'These pages will argue that pornography is an expression not of human erotic feeling and desire, not of a love of the life of the body, but of a fear of bodily knowledge, and a desire to silence eros.'[8] The *voyeur* cannot take the risk of shared life, any continued engagement, with the sex-object; the photographed body, the body in the picture on the wall, is the body that can be controlled totally, that can be observed without the threat of returning the stare.

Above all the *voyeur* must see and not feel. He keeps a safe distance. He does not perspire and his photographs do not glisten with sweat. He is not touched by reality. And yet, in his mind, he can believe he possesses reality. For he has control over these images he makes and he shapes them to his will.[9]

The *voyeur* represents in an extreme form that flight from vulnerability, the safe refuge in fantasy, that characterizes all unhealed sexuality.

'Do you not know that he who joins himself to a prostitute becomes one body with her? For, as it is written, "The two shall become one flesh" ' (v. 16). This suggests that the act of giving your body of itself implies a past and a future. It is a unity that must find expression in a shared history. To be bodily is to live in time. And one reason for the current crisis in sexual morality is that we have a weakened sense of what it means to live in time, and to find the significance of our lives realized not in an instance but in the stretch of a lifetime. This loss of a sense that our lives might have meaning as a whole, a necessary sensitivity if one is to perceive what it might mean to be a sexual being who can give one's body to someone else, has been brilliantly analysed by Alisdair MacIntyre in *After Virtue*. He points to the way in which

> modernity partitions each human life into a variety of segments, each with its own norms and modes of behaviour. So work is divided from leisure, private life from public, the corporate from the personal. Both childhood and old age have been wrenched away from the rest of human life and made into distinct realms. And all these separations have been achieved so that it is the distinctiveness of each and not the unity of the life of the individual who passes through those parts in terms of which we are taught to think and to feel.[10]

MacIntyre believes that we can only recover a proper sense of who we are and of what is virtuous by regaining some sense of our lives as wholes, which have sense as stories that reach from a birth to a death. 'To ask "What is the good for me?" is to ask how best I might live out that (narritival) unity (of my life) and bring it to completion.'[11] And so a proper sense of the sexually appropriate goes with a recovery of an awareness of how we are historical, temporal beings, who can make promises to each other, and so pledge ourselves with our bodies. As Hosea offered his contemporaries release from the merely mythological sexuality of Ba'al and his lover, the timeless repetition of spring and winter, so a proper Pauline sexual ethic heals one of the fantasy of the abstracted

moment so that we may live in time together, and so glorify God in
our bodies.

1   See J. Murphy O'Connor, 'Corinthian Slogans in 1 Cor. 6: 12–20,
    The Catholic Biblical Quarterly, Vol. 40(3), 1978, pp. 391–6.
2   This translation of 1 Cor is taken from the RSV, except that I have
    changed the location of some of the quotation marks, and altered v.
    18, which the RSV gives as 'every other sin'. The Greek is clearly
    'every sin'; the RSV alters it presumably because it can make no sense
    of the statement. When, as Murphy O'Connor claims, this is
    recognized as a Corinthian slogan, then of course it makes perfect
    sense.
3   'A Long Sermon for Holy Week – Part 3: The Easter Vigil: The
    Mystery of New Life', *New Blackfriars*, April 1986, p. 167.
4   In *Paul the Apostle: The Triumph of God in Life and Thought*, Edinburgh,
    1980, p. 287ff.
5   *Op. cit.*, p. 288.
6   An unpublished sermon to which I am deeply indebted.
7   *Op. cit.*, p. 393.
8   *Pornography and Silence: Culture's Revenge against Nature*, London, 1981,
    p. 1.
9   *Ibid.*, p. 122.
10 *After Virtue: A Study in Moral Theory*, London, 1981, p. 190.
11 *Ibid.*, p. 203.